CW00349579

Conte

This book is one of a limited edition of 1000 copies

No: 0327

As war loomed the authorities were very concerned about providing safe public air raid shelters. This was to prove a large problem. There were already schemes to supply Anderson and Morrison shelters in people's homes. In the early days some people had to pay for these – an early 'means test' – but they were later provided free. Another problem arose with shelters for school children: arguments raged regarding whether they should be on the surface or underground. In the end underground shelters were built where circumstances allowed them.

With the outbreak of war, public shelters were built, many on the surface and built of brick. One such shelter was built near Preston Circus, another at the south end of the gardens in Grand Parade.

The photograph shows children at Moulsecoomb School, Lewes Road, entering their underground shelter in November 1939 as part of their air raid shelter drill. (Brighton Local Studies Library)

War in the City

Volume 1

David Rowland

FP

Finsbury Publishing

By the same author:
The Brighton Blitz
The Coastal Blitz
Spitfires Over Sussex: the Exploits of 602 Squadron

Front cover: Brighton Municipal Clinic in Sussex Street on Monday 29th
March, 1943. Two young children were killed on the entrance steps. (*Brighton Local Studies Library*)
Back cover: Shelley Road, Hove, on 9th March, 1943. (*Author's collection*)

British Library Cataloguing-in Publication Data.
A catalogue record for this book is available from the British Library.

ISBN 0-9539392-1-9

Published by Finsbury Publishing, 2 Harvest Close, Telscombe Cliffs,
Peacehaven, East Sussex BN10 7JG

Printed by Tansleys Printers, 19 Broad Street, Seaford, East Sussex BN25 1LS

Introduction

In 1997 my first book, *The Brighton Blitz*, was published. I was amazed by its popularity. It appears that stories about the Second World War are as popular as ever and local wartime history even more so. The book told the story of a number of wartime air attacks on the town between 1940 and 1944. Some of them were already well documented, but the book contained the personal reminiscences of people who were there at the time.

I suppose the most infamous of all the German attacks on the town occurred on Saturday 14th September 1940, when a bomb exploded on the Odeon cinema in Kemp Town, killing a number of children and causing injury to many more (*page 19*). It is all so easy to write a story and naming somebody or other who has been killed, but this doesn't indicate the trauma and utter devastation caused to their family and friends. The onlooker may feel sorrow and grief at the time, but for the family it lasts for ever, with events acting as reminders for the rest of their lives.

Two other air attacks stand out in the history of the town during the Second World War, and both of these occurred within three months of each other in 1943. The first was the bombing of the Municipal Clinic in Sussex Street during the morning of 29th March (*front cover*) when a number of men, women and children lost their lives. The bomb burst through the north wall of the fruit and vegetable market in Circus Street, killing a market employee, and crossed the roadway before exploding close to the main entrance of the clinic Two children were playing on the steps while their pregnant mother was inside with a nurse: although they were killed instantly, their bodies showed no outward signs of injury. Another bomb struck tenement houses next to the Baptist Church in Gloucester Place, claiming several lives. Major damage was caused to these buildings.

There was also the terrible bombing of the town at lunchtime on Tuesday 25th May. More than 20 bombs were dropped, killing 27 people and injuring 130 more – a day when the rescue services were at full stretch, and a day that I personally shall never forget.

Over the past few years I have tried very hard to find more information about the Brighton incidents with a view to filling in the existing gaps. A few more facts and relevant information are included in this book, and my curiosity will ensure that this quest is never-ending.

What of Hove, Brighton's sister town, during those wartime years? It, too, suffered through the war, and many local people were killed and injured. I thought it about time that Hove told its story of the wartime bombings but, as with Brighton, the information is a little scarce: I am sure, however, that more material will come to light over the years. I have already received a lot of information as a result of letters printed in the *Argus* and other local publications, and Hove residents have sent me their stories, too.

Hove experienced its first air attack before Brighton, during the night of Saturday 29/30th June 1940, when two bombs were dropped on the West Hove golf course, causing a large crater and a few smashed windows.

One of the worst air attacks on Hove appears to have occurred at the same time as Brighton's 'day when the clinic was bombed'. This day is known in Hove as 'the day that the Shirley Press was bombed' – 29th March 1943, when a 16-week-old baby was killed while it lay in its pram in Shirley Street. Other areas that received direct hits in this air attack included Nizells Avenue, Colbourne Road and Clarenden Villas.

Yet another disaster had occurred a few days earlier, on the 9th March, when 12 people were killed and 33 injured. The main areas to have suffered included Shelley Road (*back cover*), Rutland Gardens and Walsingham Terrace, a concentration of bombs scoring direct hits. Several people were killed and injured in Shelley Road, including a former senior Metropolitan policeman, Thomas Divall, who was killed along with his housekeeper.

Divall is believed to have worked on the Jack the Ripper case after he was promoted to the rank of inspector and transferred to 'H' Division (Whitechapel) on 17th October 1900. Born on 16th June 1861, he joined the Metropolitan Police Force on 14th August 1882, retiring on 13th March 1913 with the rank of chief inspector. On retirement he moved to Botley, Hampshire, before moving to Hove.

Other terrible incidents came to light during the research for the book, such as the sad story of Frederick Hodgkinson. He was a retired newspaperman, having been a sub editor on the *Sussex Daily News* and editor of the *Evening Argus* many years ago. He was in Aldrington Avenue, a few doors from where his daughter lived. She was very ill at home, and he was on his way to visit her when he was killed by machine gun fire from attacking enemy aircraft.

In this book I have also taken the unusual step of publishing word for word the details of a diary kept by Brighton-born Private Laurence Seale during his time as a prisoner of war. He was held in both Italian and German camps, and I include his drawing of the first of them.

This is the first of two books that will highlight more tales of life in Brighton and Hove during the Second World War.

David Rowland
Telscombe Cliffs, 2002

In 1939, as war was declared, there were many rumours circulating, among them the belief that the county was about to be attacked with chemical and biological gases. Another fear was that the southern part of the country would be fire-bombed prior to an invasion, and this seemed rather more likely: chemical and biological attacks, after all, might prove dangerous for the German troops as they invaded. The authorities turned their minds to the method of dealing with fire-bombing. They would need many dozens of fire engines, but they had neither the time nor the money to purchase them. The solution was to adapt vehicles of any description that could be used for fire-fighting purposes – and our photograph shows one of them in Hove during 1939. (Brighton Local Studies Library)

The Start of the Second World War

The Second World War began on 3rd September 1939 – at 11am, to be precise. There had been all types of rumours about what would happen to the British People once the war had started. It seemed that just about everyone had their own ideas of what was to befall them. Most had been issued with gas masks and shown how and when to use them. Many people believed that the Germans were going to drop gas on the towns and cities. They had seen the effects this had had on soldiers during the First World War, and the horrors of that war soon came flooding back. As was often the case, rumours were

Training for a gas attack. This photograph was taken near the old Seeboard showroom in the Old Steine.

very quick to spread. Many people had adapted rooms in their homes to give them a 'safe' shelter should gas attacks occur. The government quickly attempted to dispel the many rumours, but in many people's minds the seeds had already been sown.

Days and months passed without anything happening, and people in the Brighton and Hove area started to relax, as it appeared that the threat of a gas attack had passed. The large number of children arriving as evacuees from the London area was the only reminder that the war had started.

People eagerly scanned their newspapers and listened intently to the wireless in order to glean all available information, but as 1939 came to a close and the winter months passed there was little change to the situation.

The first few months of 1940 indicated what might be in store for this country, with the German forces invading different countries, and then in May came the Dunkirk debacle. About the same time the first bombs fell on mainland Britain. (The first British casualty of enemy bombing had been killed two months before, on 24th March, when bombs fell on Hoy in the Orkneys.) On the 9th May there was an attack near Canterbury, Kent, and later that month, on the 24th, the first industrial town – Middlesborough – was targeted. This was followed in June by bombs falling in the London area for the very first time, landing in fields outside Addington, Surrey, on the 18th.

On the 30th June, the first bombs fell on Hove and just two weeks later Brighton suffered its first bomb attack. The local residents now knew without doubt that there was a war on.

Now, throughout the summer months, the Battle of Britain was played out in the skies over Sussex and Kent, with an almost daily audience of thousands. This period culminated on the 15th September 1940 when the Battle of Britain was won and the very real threat of an invasion passed.

During these times the government were forced to ration many every day foodstuffs, such as meat, bacon, eggs and cheese. – a subject covered (*page 47*) in a later chapter.

Closing the Beaches

The local newspaper dated 3rd July 1940 announced the closure of the beaches and promenades along the south coast, stretching from the eastern side of Brighton through to the western part of Selsey almost to the Hampshire border. This area (including Brighton, Hove, Worthing , Bognor Regis and scores of smaller places) was now entirely closed to the public for the foreseeable future.

The ban closed bathing, boating and paddling pools and it also had a major effect on other entertainment places such as tennis courts, bowling and putting greens. Certain pleasure gardens were also affected, and this led to a public outcry.

The district itself was not a 'prohibited area' as there were no restrictions on travel, but the sudden ban dealt a severe blow to the resort traders, and representations were being made on their behalf in the hope that there might be some relaxation. A number of shopkeepers and stallholders were put out of business almost at once. 'If we can't earn a living,' one indignant beach stall holder said, 'we certainly can't pay the council.'

A race to the beach for the last dip in July, 1940 – an Evening Argus picture.

Marine Parade after the closure of the beach, the south side of Marine Parade and Madeira Drive in July, 1940. Note the seats on the north side of marine parade.

The large seafront hotels were a little luckier and the manager of one such hotel told the local newspaper: 'The large hotels will, generally speaking be keeping open until the end of the month (July) at any rate.' He went on: 'We are hoping that when the bad weather comes, and the danger of sudden landings is correspondingly reduced, the ban may be lifted.'

Shortly before 5pm on Tuesday 2nd July 1940, soldiers in pairs, with rifles slung across their backs, walked backwards and forwards to every little group on the beach saying 'You must leave here in a quarter of an hour'. A steady stream of men, women and children began leaving the beaches and drifting onto the promenades, crossing the roads to the north side. When this had almost been completed a police car with loudspeaker attachment 'whipped up' the stragglers. When the area was completely cleared an Army lorry drove slowly along the full length of the seafront, an officer standing up to see that all was clear and taking the salute from the various groups of soldiers.

Brighton and Hove were fortunate in being able to retain their municipal swimming baths (the North Road baths in Brighton and the long established seawater baths situated on the north side of the Hove seafront), but both the Brighton Cruising Club and the Deep Sea Anglers club members had to leave their waterside premises not knowing when they might return. The fishing fraternity, bereft of their immortal 'hard', had to seek a new fishmarket. Within a short time, Mr. Avery, the superintendent of baths and markets, organised a new home for them in the Circus Street market.

Prior to this seafront ban being introduced both Brighton and Hove had had an evening curfew introduced. This meant that certain areas (mainly the streets just off the main seafront roads) were 'no go' after the fixed curfew of half an hour after sunset.

Towards the end of July 1940 the partial lifting of the evening curfew occurred. The regional commissioner announced that, following discussions held with the local military authority, the curfew would be modified for people visiting places of entertainment in the area: the curfew hour was now to be 10pm, with places of entertainment affected allowed to remain open until 9.45pm. However, the military commander emphasised the need for people to hurry home directly they left.

The chief constable, Captain Hutchinson, announced that he had further arranged that people living in the curfew area might attend any house of entertainment north of the district, provided that they were back home by 10pm. He also stated that on returning to the curfew area they might be asked to produce their 'half tickets' as evidence of their being genuine residents. The Chief Constable of Hove, Mr. William Hillier, also announced a modification of the curfew areas, with similar restrictions to those in Brighton.

The local newspaper had something of a scoop in announcing that there might be some relaxation to the restriction currently in order covering the area of the seafront and beaches. This, it would appear, applied only to a small area of beach between the two piers, but further discussions were being arranged and these were to take place over the next few weeks.

The Lower Esplanade during wartime. Note the tank traps at the bottom of the slope.

THE WAR IN BRIGHTON

Small fishing boats in Queen's Park pond, autumn 1940. They had been moved from the beach near the Banjo Groyne.

Two members of the rescue services at Princes Terrace on July 15, 1940, after the first air attack on the town. Some 180 houses were damaged in the Whitehawk area after eight 'whistling bombs' fell. (Brighton Local Studies Library)

Brighton's First Air Attack, 15th July 1940

The residents of Brighton, as in other places on the south east coast, had become rather blasé about the war. They had listened to the various wartime speeches given by the government and read the information in the newspapers. They had been informed that they would be bombed and perhaps gassed, but ten months had passed and nothing had happened. Some wondered aloud whether there was really a war on.

In the early morning of Monday 15th July, however, a big change was made to the lives of Brightonians. A distant sound of an aircraft could be faintly heard. Such sounds were not familiar to people yet, but as the war rolled on they would be almost instantly recognised by the general public, especially those charged with public safety. The men and women who were members of the different ARP squads, Home Guard and police were soon to become expert in knowing the particular engine sounds of different types of aircraft.

This day a single German bomber, a Dornier Do 17, dropped a number of bombs before flying out to sea. The incident took little more than two minutes, but it is known that the aircraft returned to the coast and dropped bombs on Hove.

The sirens were not sounded, and people therefore had no chance to find any shelter, but at that time the sirens were often sounded for practice, and it is possible that few would have responded in any case. This was the first attack on Brighton, and this part of the town would have several more air attacks before the war came to a close.

The Dornier dropped 9 small bombs, weighing 25kg (around 50 pounds) including one of the whistling type which were dropped to bring terror to the residents, and very often did. The bombs landed in Bennett Road, Bristol Gardens, Henley Road, Princess Terrace, Rugby Place and Whitehawk Road. Six houses were demolished and about 30 more seriously damaged. Approximately 180 houses over an area of about a half mile radius suffered minor damage with roof and broken glass only.

HUNDREDS HAVE AMAZING ESCAPES

A WOMAN and two men were killed, and several injured, two seriously, during a raid on two South-East coast towns this morning.

The dead woman was Mrs. Ethel Hargreaves and the dead men were Albert G. Charles and Henry May.

Among the injured were William South, George Wood and Frank Davis.

Eight bombs were dropped on one town by a Dornier which then turned out to sea, but again flew inland to drop the same number of bombs on a nearby town.

Hundreds of people had amazing escapes from wrecked bedrooms.

SCREEN SAVES BABY

One bus conductor was shaving when a piece of shrapnel missed his face by inches and embedded itself in the wall. Another house was hit by a bomb, but the two occupants, a woman and her daughter, escaped unhurt.

In the next street a bomb fell in a back garden. A baby was fast asleep in its cot as the ceiling collapsed, but the blast of the bomb had blown a draught screen over the child and saved it from injury. A cat and a sparrow were the only casualties.

An Evening Argus cutting on July 15, 1940.

The rescue squads were quickly on the scene and assisted with evacuating distressed families from their homes. Many of these went to stay with neighbours, while most of the others went to nearby relatives. A local hall was opened but in the event wasn't used. A 6-inch gas main in Whitehawk Road and a 4-inch main in Bennett Road caused small fires. These were soon brought under control, and the mains were fully repaired by late evening. A water main was also damaged in Bennett Road and repaired the same day. Bomb splinters made three holes in a cast iron distribution post at the junction of

Princess Terrace and Bristol Gardens. A short circuit was caused on two cables attached to a lamppost: a temporary service was carried out within a couple of hours. Glass was strewn across Whitehawk Road and was of some concern. The shop windows had been criss-crossed with tape to prevent flying glass, but this had not worked as every shop window was broken and strewn across the roadway.

No roads were blocked by the debris but diversions were imposed in the Whitehawk Road area. A part of Bristol Gardens was cordoned off for about three hours from the beginning of the incident. There were no UXBs recorded. Similar damage was suffered by other shops in the streets where damage had been caused.

This incident appears to have been used as a practice by the authorities as they sent five ambulances, two first aid parties, one rescue party and two sitting-case cars. It was admitted that this number was far too many for the number of casualties that occurred.

Whitehawk Road after Brighton's first air attack.

The first death occurred at 13 Princes Terrace, where the occupant, 67-year-old Ettie Hargreaves, was killed when one of the bombs hit her home. Her body was later taken to the mortuary at Hodshrove Farm. Two men were very seriously injured in Bristol Gardens, one of them outside the Clyde Arms public house. He was rushed to the Royal Sussex County hospital, where he died the following day. Meanwhile the other man died as he was being placed in the ambulance and was taken to the Royal Sussex. Four other men also suffered quite serious injuries. Bill South of 54 Wiston Road, Whitehawk and Francis Haynes of 35 Wiston Road (both believed to be postmen) were taken to the Royal Sussex, as was George Wood of 9 Maresfield Road, Whitehawk. Frank Davis of 40 Bennett Road was taken to the Sussex Eye Hospital. They later all made a full recovery.

George Allen, a former soldier, later reported that he heard the droning sound of an aircraft about 6am. 'I got up out of bed,' he said. 'The engine sound indicated that the aircraft was pretty high up. It flew around several times, probably taking about 15 minutes. I went outside and stood on the street corner it was pretty deserted, with only a few early morning workers moving about. I could still hear the engine sound of the aircraft. It was as if it had decided to target this area. I quickly dived for cover as I heard the bombs falling. They came down with a sort of whistle and then a muffled whoomph sound.

'It's difficult to say exactly what happened next as everything seemed to happen at once. What I remember the most was the area being quickly covered with clouds of dust and intermingled with sounds of breaking and flying glass. I recall people shouting for help and other people shouting that they were on their way to help. The sounds were totally mixed and I really don't know in what order they came. I went across the road and started moving pieces of wood and slates, being careful with the broken glass. The rescue services were on the scene so quick. I don't know where they came from but they appeared like magic.'

Local surveyors who attended the scene were amazed by the small number of casualties. Many windows were blown out in six streets adjoining the scene.

Another view of Princes Terrace after the air raid.

Speaking to an *Argus* reporter, a council official said 'We reckoned that we would have to provide housing for about 40 families. We were generously offered a large building with 56 bedrooms, staffed by a cook and four maids, but so many neighbours came to the rescue that we only had to put eight families there that night, and only one family remained there the following night. We were prepared to open up the schools as feeding centres but, again, friends and neighbours made this quite unnecessary. This is truly a case where the community came together in an emergency situation.

'The first aid building repair scheme was given a good test, proving a great success. By the evening of the incident, every house that could be rendered habitable was fully equipped with new windows and doors. The roofs were mended making them completely watertight again. There were 14 different building firms who did a superb job working until late in the evening to complete their tasks.

'One thing that I must stress was the spirit of the people. They have been just wonderful. There were no weeping women or crying babies. The women were cheerfully at work with brooms and dusters, clearing up the mess and sorting out the rubbish. There really is only one word for it: wonderful.'

Having dropped a number of bombs on Brighton, the German aircraft now made off over the Channel in a southwesterly direction. It then turned back and headed for Hove. A local resident recalled that the bombs appeared to be jettisoned from the plane as it was turning towards the sea. It then hurriedly made off southwards. A minute or two later a pair of fighters roared over the town in pursuit of the raider.

The brunt of the bombs hit the area of New Church Road, while houses in nearby streets also suffered severe damage. One of the bombs fell in the garden of a large empty house in New Church Road and killed Albert Charles of 37 The Gardens, Southwick. He was one of a group of Home Guard who had been on night duty in the area. Two others were severely injured and rushed to Hove General Hospital.

Men of a demolition Squad saw the salvo of bombs fall, ran to their lorries and set off towards the sound of the explosions before they received any instructions. They arrived in New Church Road as the dust was settling, to find considerable damage to properties in the Road. There were several people who needed attention for their injuries: six were transported to hospital suffering severe injuries, while two others were treated by local first aiders for facial cuts caused by flying glass.

Note: Having checked a number of books on the subject of German Aircraft losses I can find only one German bomber that failed to return from an operational mission on this day. It cannot be proved that this was the aircraft responsible for the two attacks.

A Junkers Ju 88 of II/LG1 failed to return. Two NCOs were killed and two others posted as missing. The aircraft was lost. There are no reported losses of Dorniers during this period.

The Odeon Cinema
14th September 1940

There is little doubt that the bomb dropped from a Dornier Do 217 and scoring a direct hit on the Odeon Cinema, St. Georges Road in Kemp Town, changed many people's minds about the war.

The very fact that a number of children were killed and injured on that Saturday afternoon, 14th September 1940, hardened people's resolve to stand firm, whatever the costs, against a German invasion or the bombing of their beloved town by the Luftwaffe.

It was hard for many people to believe that a single bomb on the cinema could kill 'hundreds of people'. That was the story that spread like wildfire around the town, and each time the story was told a few more killed and injured were added to the list.

When the bomb struck the cinema at around 3.40pm there was complete silence for a couple of seconds – a phenomenon often noted at other bombing incidents, the times mentioned sometimes being 'split seconds'.

Severe damage in Upper Rock Gardens/Eastern Road after the bombing raid of September 14.

This silence then changed as the clouds of dust, dirt and pieces of debris descended on the people in the audience. It was then that the fear and fright set in, as the children started to scream and cry and parents shouted for help for their children or themselves, their calls and screams getting louder all the time. The darkness added to the fear, with terrified people desperately trying to find their way out.

Two of the first people on the scene were my father and his workmate Bob Hunt. They were working across the road at the Kemp Town Brewery, and they ran across the road and into the cinema. My father later told me that they had no thought of danger at that time, but only some hours later after it was all over.

The ARP rescue teams were quickly on the scene and were soon joined by a number of doctors and nurses from the nearby Royal Sussex County Hospital at the top of Paston Place. They had realised that the Odeon cinema had been hit when they saw the smoke and clouds of dust coming from the open roof. They ran the hundred

The Odeon, Kemp Town, after the bomb damage had been repaired.
The cinema was later demolished and replaced by a block of flats.
(L. Pattenden, Brighton)

yards or so down Paston Place carrying what medical supplies they could. A local army unit soon joined the rescuers, later followed by a naval unit.

It has been estimated that there were about 300 people in the cinema at the time the bomb fell and it was surely a miracle that more people hadn't been killed or injured. There was, as we have seen, talk at the time about 'hundreds' being killed but in reality there were two children definitely killed while in the cinema: Pamela Sturgess, who was just six years old, and 15-year-old Frank Stutterford who was on duty in the cinema for the St. John Ambulance Brigade. Two adults were also killed: Edith Barton who was 62 years old and Johanna Marchant who was 55.

Although these numbers were a long way from the figures first bandied about, it must be stressed that there were many more children and adults who were either very badly injured in the cinema and died later the same day at the Royal Sussex County hospital or who were killed at the cinema but verified dead only when arriving at the hospital. The official records do not clearly state the details. What is known is that many people suffered appalling injuries and were almost certainly dead at the scene. These included the following children: Stanley Baldwin 14 years, Sidney Borrow 11 , Ivor Davies 14, Freda Harris 14, Nellie Loftus 15 and Mary Sharpe 11. The adults who died were: Alfred Chapman 18 years, Edith Mason 68 (she died at the hospital on 18th November), Lilian Rosenzweig 46 and Ronald Walker 40.

The known total of deaths attributed to the cinema bomb were eight children and six adults – a very sad total even if far short of the rumoured figures.

The cinema staff did a fine job of helping the injured people to escape and the cinema company's managing director personally thanked the local manager. All the staff was later sent away for a short holiday in recognition of their rescue work on this day.

The Odeon Cinema bomb:
June Longly remembers.

❲ In September 1940 I lived with my parents, Bill and Gladys and my younger brother Phillip at an address in Sussex Square. My father was the caretaker of a large block of flats.

On Saturday 14th September 1940 my mum, Phillip and I decided to go to the pictures at the Odeon in Kemp Town, a short distance from our home. The alternative was to go shopping but after some discussion we decided that we would like to go to the cinema although we had seen most of the film before – the reason being that a lady had taken us to the Odeon in Hove a short while before as a special treat. She also lived in our block of flats. At this time we had missed the beginning of the film and so we decided that we would like to go again when the film was shown at our local cinema. What a fateful decision this turned out to be! I have lived and re-lived this terrible day many times over during the past 60 years. It really was horrific.

I have tried very hard to write down the facts of this day but even after several attempts I cannot do it justice.

The three of us left home walking the short distance through the streets of Kemp Town. I was feeling very happy and excited as I walked along with Phillip, mum a short distance behind. The weather was fine with a rather weak sun. It had been a lovely hot summer but now the summer was slowly giving way to autumn.

We arrived at the cinema in plenty of time and had to queue. It was very busy as it usually was on a Saturday afternoon. This time was very popular with children and their parents. We went in and soon got settled in our seats.

The film was a comedy called, 'The Ghost comes Home', and we had only seen a few minutes of it when there was an enormous bang accompanied by an awful lot of noise – difficult to describe, but it was really awful. There were clouds of dust and dirt, hanging as if it was a curtain. All this happened so quick that you couldn't put a time to it. This is a memory that has stayed with me since that day; I can still see it now. I was then aware that a large part of the roof was missing. In fact the sky was clearly visible. The screen was split from top to bottom, and the dust and dirt seemed to be coming from where the torn screen was. I remember that my mouth was full of grit and dust as by this time the whole of the cinema was full of this dirty stuff floating through the air.

I remember seeing someone trapped under a large piece of the roof, calling for help, trying in vain to get out from underneath it. I was then picked up by a man and carried towards an exit, which was at the front of the cinema. It turned out that this man was related to the lady who owned and lived in the block of flats next to ours. I later learned that his name was de Haviland, and that he was a member of the famous aircraft company. We left the auditorium and went down some steps into the corridor leading to the foyer. There was a man lying on the floor. I was told not to look, but it was too late – I had seen him. He looked to be dead.

The next thing was that I was outside the cinema and was put onto a double deck bus that had been commandeered by the rescue services and was parked in the roadway just outside the cinema in Paston Place facing up towards the Royal Sussex County Hospital. My next memory is of being carried by my father and that we were in the outpatients department in Eastern Road and opposite the main hospital. I cannot remember exactly how I got to be in this position or how my father arrived there.

I saw my mother was lying on a stretcher but there was no sign of my brother, Phillip. My father was very worried about my brother and it took until 10pm for him to discover his whereabouts. He toured the various hospital wards time and time again as injured people were being brought in all the time. He was in one of the wards and my father recognised him by his pitiful crying. He was hurt and very frightened. He suffered the loss of the third finger of his right hand. The index and second fingers were so badly damaged that they were stiff and useless. He had a shrapnel wound in his thigh, and when he was eventuallydischarged from hospital he still had the shrapnel. The hospital said that it would work itself out in time. In fact after a lot of care and patience my father eventually managed to remove it. My brother kept the piece of shrapnel in a matchbox for years. He was just four and a half years old when this incident happened.

I had suffered very severe injuries that included losing half a buttock, horrible shrapnel wounds in my left leg and under my right arm. I was only seven years old and it was a total nightmare to me. Needless to say that I was very frightened and thought I might die. It was all extremely painful. I was admitted to a ward and remember lying in bed with various types of cages over my back, one of which had electric light bulbs in it. I was painted with a bright yellow liquid. When I was due to have the stitches removed from under my arm one of the nurses told me that if I didn't cry, her daughter would give me some nice beads. I cried, as it hurt, but I was given the beads. They were coloured red and yellow and I kept them for many years. I underwent many, many operations: skin grafts. I had skin removed from the back of my thigh and placed on the wounds to my buttock. I recall that I had been given a lovely double-jointed doll and somehow one of her legs had come off. I was due for yet another operation about this time, and when I came round from it there was my doll with a splint on her leg. One of the staff had mended it for me.

At this time I was in York block with my mother. It was a separate block to the right and behind the main hospital. The sister in this ward was called Sister Perkins – Polly of course. My mother later told me that for three weeks after the raid in which we were casualties I didn't speak a word. (That is probably why I was put into a ward with my mother.) One day a lady was admitted for observation and when I saw her, I said, 'I know that lady: she's my teacher.' She only stayed overnight but my mother was sure that she had been sent in to help me. I was in hospital for seven months. All that time I was lying on my stomach. Once I was discharged it took me a very long time before I could sleep any other way apart from on my stomach. Because of my skin grafts and the position of my main injury I found it very difficult to travel on buses with their itchy seat coverings – it was very uncomfortable. I used to take a cushion with me whenever we travelled. I left many cushions on the buses and lost them.

My mother's injuries were very serious, and the pain she initially suffered had to be almost totally unbearable. However, she wasn't one for complaining. Her right leg was badly damaged behind the knee and lower down. The leg muscles and nerves had been shattered. As a result of these injuries she was in and out of hospital for many years. She attended hospitals far and wide, including the Horton emergency hospital at Epsom, the Queen Victoria hospital at East Grinstead and the Queen Elizabeth hospital at Roehampton. She would be sent home in between times and then re-admitted for more operations. At one stage she had a calliper fitted. Finally in 1946, six years after the raid and after the numerous operations that she had endured, it was decided that the leg could not be saved and it was amputated. Thinking back now she certainly went through a lot, and how my poor father coped I just don't know, but he did. There was of course no such thing as counselling in those days. The hospital matron told my father that if they want to talk about it, then let them. That, as it happened, turned out to be sound advice.

My brother and I grew up as normal children despite the terrible incident that involved us on that Saturday afternoon. Maybe we should have gone shopping after all! ,

THE LIGHTER SIDE OF WAR 1

Scanning old newspapers for wartime information one often comes across the humour shared by people at this dark period of their lives. It is easy to understand the need for light relief after bombs have been raining down night after night. For the government, meanwhile, it was essential to keep the morale of the public high throughout the years of the war. Here and elsewhere are some vignettes from the newspapers of the time.

Cigarette Smoking: August 7th 1940.

Police have declared war on roof squatters who smoke cigarettes during air raid warnings.

A spokesman stated: 'These pests are causing the authorities great trouble and they must be heavily punished. During the last few night warnings scores of people have rushed into police stations to report 'spies on roof tops- signalling to the enemy'. Police officers have invariably found that the 'spies' are careless sightseers who have climbed onto rooftops and are sitting there blissfully puffing away at cigarettes and striking matches. They are indignant when they are told they are forming a dangerous landmark. This practice must be stamped out. The police have instructions to deal severely with offenders. They will be summoned for 'showing naked lights', and heavy punishments will be asked for.

Two days after the above report appeared in the newspapers, this one appeared.

Offender

An officer of the Home Guard, Owen Simmonds, was fined 10s.6d for permitting a 'glow' of a cigarette to be visible in the street while an air raid warning was in operation.

It was explained in 'Official Circles' that it is an offence against the 'lighting regulations'. If you are caught in a raid with a lighted cigarette you should put it out immediately.

20th September 1940

Around midday on Friday 20th September 1940, the wailing sirens indicated another air attack and almost immediately the drone of aircraft engines were heard. People scattered in fright, searching for the nearest shelter, and just as some was lucky enough to find the minimum of shelter, bombs started to fall.

One scored a direct hit on the Franklin Arms in Lewes Road (later called The Lewes Road Inn). This all but destroyed the pub and killed a number of people inside. Another bomb fell on terraced houses in Caledonian Road demolishing three of these houses. Others nearby were extensively damaged.

Rescuers at the Franklin Arms public house in Lewes Road, later called the Lewes Road Inn. The licensee and his barmaid were rescued, but two people were killed. (Cissy Johnstone, Hove)

The clearest memory for many people who were in the area at the time was the huge amount of black coal dust, clouds of brick dust and a large amount of feathers floating about in the air – the feathers coming from the mattresses that were popular around this time. A dramatic rescue was centred on the Franklin Arms as large numbers of rescue workers descended on the incident. It was fortunate that the public house was not too busy at this time: another hour, and the number of customers might well have been doubled.

As the rescuers worked at moving the huge amount of rubble, a faint voice could be heard. It was Betty Marchant, the barmaid, but it took close on two hours to reach her. She had been serving behind the bar when the bomb struck, and as she fell to the floor the bar had collapsed over her: this somehow protected her from falling debris. She was eventually released from the debris three hours after the bomb fell. She was brought out pale and weak, and when a friend called out to her she managed to respond with a faint wave prior to being taken to the hospital.

The work continued– and the rescuers were soon rewarded when they found the licensee, badly injured but alive.

James Frew

This is the story of a WWII professional soldier who, while on leave in Brighton was killed during an air attack on the town. Mrs. Kathleen Ward, his sister-in-law, has related the story to me.

❰ James Frew was a Quarter Master Sergeant, serving in the Royal Sussex Regiment in 1940. He had joined the army quite a while before the war, and had seen service in Belfast and Egypt. He had married Gertie in the mid 1930s, and they had an 18-months -old daughter Jeanne born just before the war started.

James was born in Brighton and knew the town well, and while on leave he stayed with his wife and my parents-in-law at no. 20 Hastings Road. In May 1940 he was serving in France with his unit and was evacuated through the French port of Brest at the same time as the Dunkirk evacuation.

During the morning of Friday 20th September 1940, which happened to be the last day of James's leave, he went for a walk along the seafront with his wife and baby daughter, Jeanne. They returned from the seafront during the late morning, heading along Lewes Road on their way to Hastings Road. He told Gertie to go home with the baby as he was having a farewell drink in the Franklin Arms. He met my husband Bill, who declined the

James and Gertie Frew.

offer as we were moving two days later and we were up to our eyes in packing. He said Cheerio to him and said that they would meet up on his next leave for a drink.

My husband walked home and had just got to the front door of our house in Quebec Street when there was a large explosion as a bomb fell. We looked out across the town towards the Lewes

James Frew's military gravestone in Bear Road Cemetery.

Road area and could see smoke rising from where the bomb had fallen. We were afraid that the bomb had hit my in-laws house in Hastings Road, and we ran to see what had happened. We were very fearful of what we might find.

We got down onto the Lewes Road and as we hurried northwards and approaching the Franklin Arms we could see that the pub had received a direct hit from the bomb. The rescue workers were there and it was very chaotic but soon we realised that Jim had been killed. In fact it seemed impossible that anyone could be pulled out and still be alive.

In fact, one survivor was pulled from the wreckage – the barmaid, Betty Marchant. She later said that James had just ordered his drink and she was in the process of getting it for him when the bomb fell. A ceiling beam came down and caught him a glancing blow on the side of his head.

All the bodies from the pub were taken to the mortuary, which at that time was in The Avenue, Moulescoomb. My husband, Bill and I went to the mortuary to identify James's body. He did not have a mark on him except for a pad on the side of his head where the beam had caught him.

He was later buried in the Bear Road Cemetery, in a military grave. I didn't go to the funeral as I looked after my niece, Jeanne.

A footnote to this story is that, although he was a serving so-ldier, the army refused his wife a widow's pension because he was in civvies when he died. However, the Royal British Legion took up his case and she was eventually awarded one. **)**

24th September 1940

It was about 3.30pm on a sunny Tuesday afternoon, when children were happily playing their games in the streets and neighbours idly talking on the doorsteps, as was the fashion in those war-torn days.

This tranquillity was soon broken when the drone of an enemy aircraft, a Junkers Ju 88, was heard. It circled around for a few minutes, and several people were pointing upwards to it. No sirens had been sounded, and so the neighbours continued to talk and the children carried on with their games. The altitude of the aircraft then dropped, and as the aircraft came lower a stick of bombs was seen. The children quickly cleared the streets, the neighbours hurrying indoors. The bombs fell in the Albion Hill area of Brighton with devastating force. At this time of the war any of the bombs that fell could inflict great fear and damage.

Bomb damage in Albion Hill, 24th September 1940. The picture shows the north side. No. 18 was a confectioners, while the shop next door was Mitchell's, the grocers.

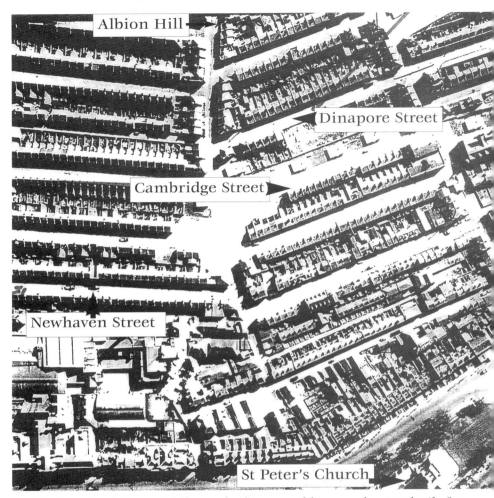

Albion Hill

Dinapore Street

Cambridge Street

Newhaven Street

St Peter's Church

The bombs fell on tightly packed terraced houses, homes built for the working class at the turn of the century. The worst damage was caused to Albion Hill, Cambridge Street and Ashton Street. Almost 30 houses were demolished or had to be demolished shortly after the attack. One of the bombs fell on a butcher's shop in Albion Hill and the junction with Ashton Street, killing the shop owner, William Chubb. Almost opposite in another of the small shops that abounded in Albion Hill was 57 year-old Nellie Vincent, at no. 13. Rescuers dug through the debris and after some hours she was pulled out, badly

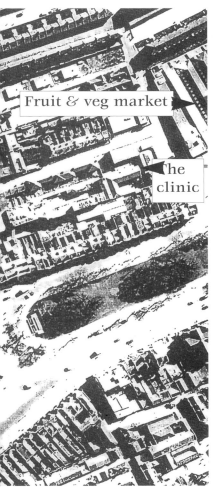

Fruit & veg market

The clinic

An aerial view of the area taken a few years after the war ended.

The damaged and semi-demolished houses were eventually removed and the area stayed derelict for some years. The eastern side of Cambridge Street then had a number of 'prefabs' erected to help with the housing shortage. These small dwellings were warm and comfortable and quickly erected. They were only supposed to be used for about five years, but they lasted a lot longer than that.

The photograph clearly shows the Cambridge Street prefabs. The large white spaces in Albion Hill show where the bombs fell and where the badly damaged and demolished houses were cleared away. Dinapore Street can also be seen, and the area where the bomb fell there is clearly visible.

injured, from the wreckage of her home and shop. She was quickly placed in an ambulance and rushed to the hospital in Elm Grove, where she died later that day.

The second bomb landed in the rear garden of the houses on the east side of Cambridge Street and wrecked many houses in that street and also in Dinapore Street.

The devastating effect caused by an exploding oil bomb was seen for the very first time in Brighton when one scored a direct hit on houses in Cambridge Street at the junction with Albion Hill. This covered a large number of houses with oil, but fortunately this bomb caused no major fires, although a number of small ones did occur. A number of streets were cordoned off while the rescue work continued.

Incredible as it may seem, only two people lost their lives in this incident, although a number of people did suffer injuries, including some children who had been playing in the nearby streets. Some of them were taken to both of Brighton's main hospitals, the Royal Sussex County Hospital and Brighton General at Elm Grove.

Lewes Street, Albion Hill, on 24th September 1940. The newsagents shop was no. 13.

14th October 1940

The air attack of Monday 14th October 1940 has bothered me for quite some time because so little is known about it.

A single bomb was dropped by a lone aircraft and struck houses in Scarborough Road, Preston Park. Serious damage was caused to the homes of several people and A 10-year-old boy lost his life (Charles Henry Siddall, who lived at no. 14) and serious damage was caused to a number of houses – and that is all that is known of this incident. I cannot link it with any other air attack in our local towns or find any further details about it.

We do know that there was an air attack in Hove at 8.10pm on this day, when 4 high explosive bombs, an oil bomb and a number of incendiary bombs were dropped, and perhaps this aircraft was responsible. I know, too, that at about 10pm a lone aircraft dropped a number of incendiary bombs and two oil bombs on the downs near the Belle Tout, near Eastbourne. Otherwise, nothing.

Houses in Scarborough Road, Preston Park, after the bomb fell.
(B. Bradbury, Brighton)

THE LIGHTER SIDE OF WAR 2

Two items from August 12th 1940.

Noisy Radios

Police will now prosecute residents who let their radio sets make
too much noise. Instructions were given to local
superintendents. Cautions will be given to offenders, but
if these are disregarded, prosecutions will follow.

Cream off.

The cream is to be skimmed off our luxuries, literally, after
October 1st. The sale of cream will be prohibited; the Ministry of
Food announced last night. The idea is to conserve liquid milk
supplies. About 70,000 gallons a year will be diverted to other
purposes.

The National Milk Scheme, it is stated, should remove any
hardship to people accustomed to obtaining scalded milk, a by-
product of the manufacture of clotted cream.

And there will be no Guy Fawkes Day either — the Ministry of
Supply prohibits from today the manufacture of indoor fireworks.

9th March 1941

About 11pm on Sunday 9th March 1941 on a bright, clear moonlight night the drone of an enemy aircraft could clearly be heard above the town. A few seconds later, the night air was shattered by a screaming sound as a number of bombs fell in the Preston village area. Witnesses claimed that 11 bombs fell on the sleeping inhabitants of the village. These bombs caused loss of life as well as serious damage to business and residential properties.

The bombs fell in Preston Road, Lauriston Road, North Road, Home Road and Cumberland Road. One bomb fell on the main Preston Road, just north of the junction with Preston Drove and almost opposite the bowling greens. This bomb fractured the gas main and caused a large fire. The nearby church, St. John's, suffered severe blast damage, with walls being demolished and cracked. A stained glass window was shattered and the church door was also damaged.

Another bomb scored a direct hit on the butcher's shop at 229 Preston Road, above which Fred and Madge Colbourne lived with their three children, Stella, Bill and Bernard. The bomb took out the front part of the building and all but Stella plunged through two floors and were buried by debris in the basement. She, however, was asleep in the back bedroom and managed to get to the window and shout for help.

The rescue services were soon on the scene and were faced with a mountain of debris knowing that somewhere beneath all this was a family of four. The only sound that could be heard was little Bernard crying, but after a further subsidence the crying stopped. After more than two hours the family were reached. The two little boys, who had been in bed together, were taken to the hospital, but Bernard was already dead. Mr. Colbourne suffered a fractured pelvis, while his wife was lucky to escape with cuts and bruises. However she was suffering severe shock, and both were taken to hospital.

A number of other shops along the main road also suffered severe damage and other rescues took place at these premises. John Stone who lived with his wife above the shop at No. 225 Preston Road was found to be dead in the debris while his wife, although badly injured, was rescued and rushed to hospital.

Several incendiary bombs were also dropped and were responsible for a number of small fires in the same area. None of these fires developed into anything serious, being quickly extinguished by the residents or by a fire service that attended in strength.

This was a long hard night for the ARP, who were pleased to see daylight and, in most cases, to be relieved by other rescue workers.

The interior of a house hit by a bomb – in this case in Scarborough Road. (See page 35.)

Violet Pumphrey's story

❨ My war began in 1938. I was just 12 years of age, and I moved from Brighton to Chelsea, London. Everywhere you went there were signs of the impending declaration of war. I can recall the endless number of sandbags being filled and made ready for use; air raid shelters were being erected in a number of places. I was issued with a gas mask, which was horrible to wear, and then to my total dismay I found out that my name was put forward at school for evacuation to Canada.

Crying, I said to my mother, after finding this out, 'What about you?' I was so unhappy at the thought of us being parted. She put on a brave face and said, 'Don't worry about me, I'll be all right.' I didn't know at this time, but in the First World War she had volunteered for the gunpowder sheds at Woolwich Arsenal. Hitler certainly couldn't scare her.

I wandered about very unhappy, my face sad and long. The thought of going to Canada kept coming back to haunt me. I was worried as well as scared: I wanted to stay here with my mum. My mum saw that I was very unhappy and I am sure that that upset her as well. One day, completely out of the blue she said, 'I have a good idea. Would you like to go back to Brighton, duck?' At first it didn't sink in, but when it did – wow! I was overjoyed. I was so happy and couldn't wait to get back to Brighton.

The south coast then was considered a safe place. In fact those kids not going abroad were evacuated there to stay with the local families. I believe it to be true that should a family have room they were bound to take in the evacuated children.

We moved back and I went back to my old school, Coleridge Street, Hove. I have only vague memories of air raid drills, going to the playground shelters when attacks were expected. I was bathing in the sea when the first air raid siren was sounded. There were quite large numbers of people on the beaches at this time. The summer of 1940 was very hot and we had lovely weather. The mothers on the beach shouted to their children and the beach cleared like magic, it was incredible. I didn't bother to dry myself, but ran home to Ventnor Villas as fast as I could where mum was waiting on the steps, looking very worried indeed. There was a buzz of excitement in the air but we went down to check on the lady who lived in the basement. We found her in the coal cellar with her gas mask on. Nothing we said would induce her to come out from her cellar. I could sympathise with her, as we just didn't know what to expect – waves of German bombers, gas attacks or something even worse.

I left school at Easter 1940 just before Dunkirk fell and although I didn't fully understand the full impact, I remember being scared that the Germans would now invade us from the

Sandbagging of the lower promenade west of the Palace Pier in the early months of the war. (Brighton Local Studies Library)

French coast. I seem to recall leaflets being issued instructing householders what to do if enemy troops came to the door. One rule was 'Do not give them food'. Were they kidding – with a gun to your head?

The summer moved on, and it was September 1940 when I felt we were really at war. I can clearly remember that night after night we would lie in bed and listen to the waves of enemy bombers overhead as they made their way to London. It was the Blitz. Mum would worry so much as her family and friends were there. She would say, 'Tch! Tch! Those poor devils, they're getting it again'. Another memory I have was the awful racket of the anti-aircraft guns firing, but I don't know if it was on these occasions. Sometimes the air raid sirens would last all night. The 'All Clear' wouldn't sound until daylight hours: it seemed that they went on for ever. Then at other times there would be no siren, the planes coming in so fast and low there just wasn't the time to take cover. These types of attacks were aimed at us, not London.

One day, on my journey to work, I was shocked to see my first bombed-out house. It was after a direct hit in Norfolk Square. It had its funny side, too, of course. One day there were six of us on the top floor of Stafford's department store, Western Road (which was the shop where I worked in the stock room) when we heard the sound of a plane, then the whistle of a bomb. We made for the stairs in double quick time and crashed down them like a herd of elephants, through the café on the floor beneath us on our way to the ground floor. I can still see the startled looks on the faces of the patrons in the café. They were half way out of their seats, wondering if they should join us. Mind, it was all too late by now; as the bomb had already exploded. The momentum carried us on until we realised what a comic lot we must have looked, and we collapsed in fits of uncontrollable laughter downstairs.

Another time, in another job, at the warning whistle of a bomb, we all dived under the desk, banging heads on the way and emerging shamefaced when the danger had passed. We always finished up shrieking with laughter, but it could also have been part hysteria. I think that was the time when a plane came down

41

near our works and we went up to gawp at it in our lunch hour, cheering, too, until we found out that it was 'one of ours', a British pilot who had tried to defend us. It was an awful feeling.

I joined the Junior Air Cadets, wore a blue blouse and a forage cap, in which I quite fancied myself. We drilled in Hove Park and were put through our paces by boy cadets, all making sheep's eyes at each other. They made me a lieutenant, even though I made a right hash of drilling the squad by myself. They must have been really hard up to promote me and, anyway, I still don't know what we were for.

I began going out with friends at night, nearly always in Brighton. Mum was a real sport allowing me out. Even though she must have really worried about the raids, she never stopped me. Selfishly, I didn't give her natural anxiety any thought, as in the same way I didn't concern myself with the rationing. I am pretty certain now that she went without just so as I could have extras.

We girls were nearly all 'second-hand Roses'. New clothes were not only a problem because of the rationing coupons, but we didn't have the money anyway. In the summertime we would paint our legs with cocoa and then draw a line up the back with a pencil so that it looked like we were wearing stockings with a seam up the back of our legs. That was all right until it rained. Ugh! Make-up was almost non-existent. The word would go around that such and such a shop had received a quota, and we would rush around there and join a queue, and hopefully be lucky and get some. It worked out that most times we would be unlucky. Is this why I have wrinkles today?

As the war went on Brighton became choc-a-bloc with troops, all kids although not many Yanks (American soldiers), so we all had plenty of partners at the many dances we went to. The Dome was the most popular with us after the Regent, and later the Aquarium. We didn't go to Sherry's in West Street, which was out of bounds for us: it had a bad name, but I don't know why. It seemed to me that the troops were gentlemen, just lonely, and they could see that you were a 'nice' girl, so I had no problems when I walked home. However, there was a murder that took place during this period. A girl's body was found in West Street. She lived locally, and the offender turned out to be a Canadian soldier. I don't know if he was sent home to do his prison sentence, although it probably was the death sentence in those days. Later, I think an American was hanged in this country having been convicted for murdering a girl.

As well as going dancing we also liked to go to the cinema. We had plenty of these in Brighton during those days. They had been built with beautiful interiors and just had something lovely about them, wonderful atmosphere, unlike the functional boxes of today. In the very early days of the war, when the sirens sounded, the film would stop and the manager would come out onto the stage and announce the fact. He would say, 'You are as safe here as anywhere'. Some people would then leave, while others stayed and then the film would continue. Eventually this was stopped and all that happened was a message flashed on the screen ,'sirens sounding', and then shortly afterwards another message, 'pips sounding' (indicating raiders overhead) and then, hopefully not too long after, 'All Clear'. That was greeted by sighs of relief all round. It was quite difficult to concentrate on the film, knowing that the sirens had sounded.

The beach was eventually put out of bounds, and so in the summertime we used to cycle out into the country. By this time all the signposts had been removed and I don't really remember quite how we managed without them. The roads in general were nearly deserted, apart from tanks and other military vehicles, although there were some civilian vehicles around.

One night when I was at a local dance hall in Brighton we were having a pretty bad air raid. I was told that a lady wished to speak to me in the foyer. This didn't make sense and so, puzzled, I made my way to the foyer, to find my Mum there. I was very annoyed at the time to see her there. She had come to meet me because of the air raid and I wasn't very grateful. Poor Mum, she had come all the way from Hove, during this air raid to see me home safely, and she was rewarded by my moaning and black looks. A boy at the dance had asked me if he could walk me to the bus stop, daring stuff in those days, so I made Mum go on alone in front of us. We were walking rather slowly and when we reached the bus stop, there was Mum at the front of the queue. To give her her due, she ignored me. I can now fully understand her anxieties, now that I am a lot older.

We eventually moved to Apollo Terrace in Brighton, and that made me very happy as it was the centre of all that was involved with having a good time, including the Brighton Girls Club, near Carlton Hill. I think this was towards the end of the summer 1942, as about six months later the Brighton clinic was bombed and our house caught some of the blast. I was on my way home after work, walking towards Sussex Street (now Morley Street) and was stopped by a warden. The clinic was a mess. I had heard rumours about the clinic, and at this time a bomb had exploded near where I worked in Hove. I explained the situation and the warden let me through. I was half frightened to go home for fear of what I might find. Luckily mum had been at work and so everything was all right. Had it been a night raid it may have been a lot different. We didn't have an air raid shelter and very rarely got up when a raid was in progress. I looked at our damaged house and when I checked inside I found that my bed was covered with broken glass, the eiderdown so badly damaged that it was a write-off. It was an old house, and the roof had to be covered with a tarpaulin until the repairs could be carried out.

That summer, 1943, we had to be housed in Whitehawk, and we had a Morrison table shelter, making us feel a lot safer. We were lying in this shelter when St. Cuthman's Church was severely damaged after a direct hit by a bomb during a night attack. We were living just across from the church, but on this occasion we had no damage.

In 1944, I went with two friends to 'Dig for Victory' in a 'far away place' – Hassocks. There was a great shortage of labour at this time, and we were encouraged to have a holiday on the land. I have to say that I have never worked so hard in my life as I did then. It was back-breaking work, tasks for which we were paid the princely sum of 30 shillings (£1.50p) for the weeks work. We were charged the same amount for our bed and board, and so we gained nothing. In fact having paid our train fare, we were out of pocket.

Around about this time the buzz-bombs or doodlebugs had started to make their appearance,and without the buildings of the towns we had a very good view of these things as they flew overhead. To me it was really weird to think that there were no pilots in these things – quite scary too.

Although I had registered for call-up when I was seventeen and was likely to be in the next group, my firm had become 'essential works' and that meant I wouldn't have to leave home, for which I am sure Mum was very pleased. I continued to enjoy myself in Brighton, travelling from Whitehawk most nights. It was easy getting into the town but difficult getting home. You couldn't use a night bus unless you were in an essential job and carried a pass.

I used to have to walk home, until one day I met up with an old friend in Hove. She had one of these passes for her job, which by then she had then left, and so gave it to me. The fact that it originally was made out for travel between Western Road (Churchill Square area) through to Hove, and that I used it to travel between Castle Square and Whitehawk, was a problem that made me nervous when I had to show it – usually by the aid of torchlight, thankfully. I could have been in very serious trouble had I been detected. **)**

THE LIGHTER SIDE OF WAR 3

Daily Express:18th August 1940.

Patience

An air raid warden on his beat called down a big shelter 'Everyone all right?' The people had been there for three hours. Up came the answer, 'All right, pal, We've got a
lovely easy chair here. We're taking turns in it — half an hour each. My turn comes next Thursday week.'

8d Meal too large.

Lady Woolton, wife of the Minister of Food, paid 8d for her midday meal, but found the first course of shepherd's pie, new potatoes and runner beans so satisfying that she had to refuse the fresh plum pudding and custard which followed.

She was visiting the new Wartime Feeding Centre opened in Dalgarno Gardens, Wormwood Scrubs, where 300 mothers, factory workers and children are fed daily at a cost of 8d for grown ups and 4d for children. The centre is self-supporting.

A middle-aged woman rescued from her badly damaged home said to one of the policemen involved, 'Will you go to the first floor bedroom and get my corsets, as I don't feel
comfortable without them?' These were the first words she uttered as she was pulled out into the sunshine. 'Got them for her,' the policeman stated.

Wartime Rationing

Apart from dodging the falling bombs and machine gun fire from enemy aircraft, the British wartime family suffered a further problem – the rationing of foods, including eggs, bacon and fats. Not all foods were placed on ration at the same time, new items being introduced gradually. The quantities of some foodstuffs were slightly adjusted from time to time after being placed on the ration.

The first stage of wartime rationing was introduced in January 1940, when bacon, ham, sugar and butter were rationed. This came, as a severe blow to housewives and families and at first was very difficult to be able to adjust to. These items were rationed as follows, per person per week: bacon (4ozs.), ham (4ozs.) sugar (8ozs.) and butter (2ozs.). Although they had been warned about the rations, people found the amounts very small.

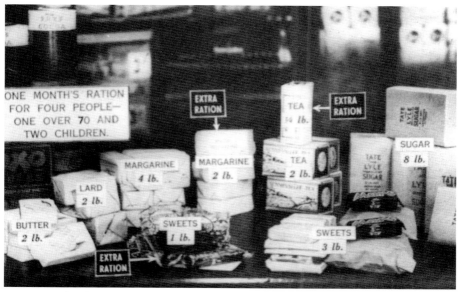

Never so healthy – but here is one family's allowance of fat, sugar and sweets for a month. Fresh milk and meat were also on 'the ration', while other foods such as bread, fish, fruit and offal were not rationed but were in short supply.

You had to laugh. This butcher certainly had a sense of humour, advising customers that 'your fresh meat ration has again been reduced' and advertising for a magician or illusionist for the following week's trade.

Matters were made worse when meat came to be rationed. The value per person per week, introduced in March 1940, was 1s.2d. More items were rationed in the July, and once again this hit the already stretched families hard. In the middle of a very hot summer the 'cuppa' came to be rationed, just 2 ozs of tea a week for each person: that was really hard to swallow. During the same month, margarine (4ozs), cooking fat (4ozs, later dropping down to 2 ozs) and cheese (2ozs at first, although it did rise to 4 ozs later) were added to the list. There was no further rationing during the remainder of 1940, and this led some misguided people to believe that nothing else would be rationed.

During the final months of 1940 the government wanted to add preserves to the items already on the ration, but they were strongly advised to leave these items for a few months, fearing that the public would not accept further items being rationed.

In March 1941 it was announced that all types of preserves would be strictly rationed – a 1lb (one pound) jar every two months for each person. This was very unpopular: children loved jam sandwiches. June saw the rationing of eggs and, again, this was a very strict ration. With distribution needing to be controlled, people were allowed one shell egg per week each if they were available – but there were many times when the distribution was one shell egg per person every *two* weeks. Later during the war dried egg was introduced: one packet every four weeks. This was a real help at eking out the miserly ration. Milk was plentiful at this time, but in November it was placed under control to about three pints per person per week, and at various times of the year during the rest of the war it was reduced to two pints. However, household (skimmed, dried) milk was available, and like the dried egg was a great help to family households.

During this time sweets, but not chocolate so much, were freely available and children continued to enjoy plentiful supplies until they too were subject to rationing. This occurred in July 1942, the ration being 12ozs per person per 4 weeks.

In addition to rationing there was a points system. Each person was allocated 16 points, and these could be used on foodstuffs as you wished. For example, your 16 points allowed you to buy one can of fish or meat, two pounds of dried fruit or eight pounds of split peas. Canned fruit was also available on the points system.

Babies and young children, together with expectant and nursing mothers, had concentrated orange juice and cod liver oil. These items were collected from the local welfare clinics together with priority milk. The milk was also allocated to invalids.

The public were required to re-register for rationed foodstuffs at shops of their choice twice a year, but you could change to another shop if you wished, instead of re-registering at the same shop. The points system was copied from a very successful scheme that had been introduced by Sainsbury's some time before.

School meals

School meals were first introduced during the war years to ensure that children had at least one hot and nutritious meal each day. Many women were working long hours in factories and other employment linked to the war effort. This was part of the Vitamin Welfare Scheme designed and introduced in December 1941, and it played a large part in ensuring that children grew up to be strong and healthy. School meals were an essential part of catering, and for many children they afforded a real treat. By February 1945 more than 1.8 million school meals were being served daily.

Meals away from home.

By the end of 1944, it was estimated that around 9 per cent of all food in Britain was consumed outside the home. There were about 150,000 catering establishments serving a little under 23 million daily meals, a staggering number. They played a very important part in supplementing the rations, as no ration cards or coupons had to be given up.

About 2,000 'British Restaurants' were opened in towns and cities around Britain. The food was relatively inexpensive and was comparable to good school dinners. It was also compulsory for factories to provide canteens, and by the end of 1944 there were more than 30,000 in existence.

In addition to these places, restaurants of all kinds were open, but it was illegal to charge more than five shillings (25p) per meal, although large and expensive establishments were allowed to make 'cover charges'.

Extra rations
Those engaged in especially heavy work were entitled to additional food, and munitions workers were allowed extra meat. Agricultural workers who could not avail themselves of canteen facilities were allowed an extra cheese ration.

Emergency feeding
After a bomb attack, gas, electric and water facilities were often out of action and the homeless had to be fed and sheltered. Mobile kitchens were organised and rushed to the scene of the bombed areas. Volunteers from the WVS and ARP workers quite often manned these mobile kitchens. They organised the food supplies as

While some foods were rationed, others – usually luxury items – were the subject of a points system. In February 1943 tinned fruit fell into this category

well as offering sympathy. There were always ample cups of tea, coffee, sandwiches and quick meals. Groups of vehicles were gathered and formed into a convoy, and they would hasten as a group to the more serious incidents. These were given top priority on the roads and called the Queen Messenger Convoys. It was essential for these vehicles to move around to the different areas quickly in order to facilitate their services.

Volunteers and emergency workers

Most people worked very hard, together with very long hours, in a large variety of jobs. These people also took part in voluntary activities, such as ARP and WVS work. There was also an army of fire watchers who spent many hours during the night time on the roofs of many important buildings, as well as those where they worked during the daytime. These emergency workers were often among the very first at the scene of incidents.

In this modern world the medical profession and nutritionists claim that we were healthier during the days of rationing than we are today, but are we? One thing was certainly true in those days: our emotions played a significant part in keeping people going. Those of us at home could not let down our armed forces, as we had a part to play, too.

The ARP (Air Raid Precaution Service) volunteers were on duty 24 hours a day, working in shifts, and often took calculated risks

In July 1940 after tea and fats were placed on ration the Food Minister, Lord Woolton, said: 'There is no shortage likely of food; nobody will go hungry.'

The time for vague appeals for economy had gone:'I am stopping luxurious feeding,' he declared.

'I am asking you for a hard life, We're going to win this war. We're going to win it by hard fighting and to fight hard we must live hard.

'We must live disciplined lives: that's what I am asking of you. No - imposing on you.'

during the rescue of trapped and injured people. Harrods, the famous department store in London, had its own ARP organisation, totalling some 700 people. These included control officers, senior pickets, permanent pickets, wardens, fireguards and women civil defence services. This was apart from their well-trained staff: they also boasted of their own firemen and special police.

Staff shortages

One of the problems that food shops in particular experienced was the shortage of staff as the war began. For example, at Sainsbury's it was obvious that the male employees would soon be called up for war service, and they lacked sufficient female staff to take over. However, they were better prepared than during the First World War. The company took the initiative and sent out thousands of letters to former female staff. They were instructed to take this letter to the manager at their nearest Sainsbury's branch, guaranteeing them re-engagement terms. It was felt that these women already had the knowledge of the very high standards that the company expected. Even this idea didn't bring in enough staff, as many women were evacuated with their children from London and the south east. A number of other women felt unable to make a long-term commitment due to the uncertain war situation.

From the middle of 1940 a variety of short courses was introduced at the company's headquarters at Blackfriars in London in order to ensure as far as possible that high standards could be maintained. This policy did mean that staffing levels rose rapidly during the first few months of the war, while the company's wage bill increased by £100,000 per week. The problem was made worse by the fact that conscription proceeded far slower than was expected. Further difficulties were encountered in employing women, as they were subject to different regulations under existing employment legislation. The 1912 Shops Act, for example, required that women should be provided with seats behind the counters. Since men had operated many of the Sainsbury's branches, such seating was often unavailable. Managers were therefore advised to make do with wooden corned beef boxes and padding covered with material. During the years from 1940 to 1943 there were just about sufficient

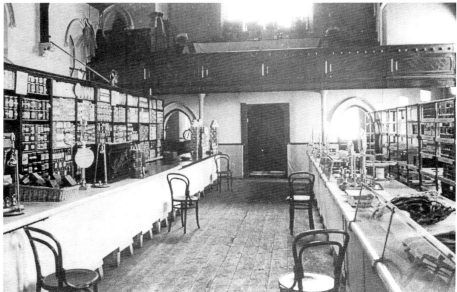

Soldiering on. After the Sainsbury's East Grinstead shop was bombed on 9th July 1943, a local church was requisitioned instead. (J. Sainsbury Archives)

staff to run the various branches, but by July 1943 staffing levels had become dangerously low. Senior management sent letters to their district supervisors stating that staff should be dismissed only as a last resort, and that a greater effort was to be made to keep existing staff. About this time the company recognised that women working full-time had difficulty in doing their shopping, and a discretionary 'shopping time' allowance of one hour per fortnight was therefore granted to full timers. In April 1944 this became a right to all women over the age of 18 years. At this time the country was being hit by flying bombs, and when many of the schools had to be closed, married women were allowed to bring their children to work.

Wartime also saw some of the very strict Sainsbury's rules relaxed. In October 1941 permission was granted for women to dispense with wearing stockings (by then very scarce and precious) during business hours. A further change in the rules occurred during a particularly cold snap in November 1943, when women were allowed to wear slacks and 'woollies' under their overalls. They were also allowed to wear warm bootees instead of shoes.

As the war progressed Sainsbury's was feeling the pinch. By March 1942 turnover was only 65% of what it had been in 1939, and it became a serious concern for those at the head of the company. They issued guidelines to the shop managers, and a notice was displayed in a prominent position in each shop. A small excerpt is printed below.

Air Raid Warnings

This shop will remain open for business until such time as the manager at his absolute discretion considers it necessary for those on the premises to take cover. Customers then in the shop will be welcome, at their own risk, to take cover with the staff.

Telephone Orders

We shall be grateful if, in accordance with the government's request, our customers will refrain from telephoning our branches during periods when an Air Raid Warning is on.

Many of the Sainsbury's branches were badly damaged during the war, in particular those in the East End of London. One branch in Watney Street had to be closed when an unexploded bomb crashed through the wall from the adjacent Maypole Dairy and settled in the foundations. The branch at East Grinstead was totally destroyed during one particular raid on the town. (*See page 54.*) On many occasions when their branches were either closed or badly damaged they moved shop, either to another nearby building or from the back of one of their vehicles – and, in extreme cases, even out in the streets. The theme of 'customer care' was certainly stretched during these years.

In the very early part of the war when there was a real threat of an invasion from the enemy, Sainsbury's actually made preparations for an invasion. Detailed instructions were sent out from head office to all branches within a 30-mile radius of the coast. In the event of an invasion staff at Folkestone, Hythe and Ashford were to go to Tonbridge, while those from the Brighton branches were to go to Haywards Heath. Each of the managers was instructed to requisition one of the branch vans for his family, and taking with him all ledgers, cashbooks, registration particulars and cash. The head office memo, anticipating that this might not be quite as simple as it sounded, added, 'If transport was commandeered, you must do your best to persuade the powers that be of the necessity of keeping your own transport to move goods from the shop which would be of value to the enemy. If the roads are blocked you must use your own initiative'

The end of rationing
Just as foodstuffs had been gradually introduced into the rationing system, so, once the war had ended, the various food items were gradually taken off it. People had imagined that food rationing would finish as soon as the war was over, but of course that was far from the truth. If we accept that the points system was a form of rationing, it's a remarkable fact that restrictions were in operation for almost 14 years – that is, from their introduction in 1940, right up to June 1954, when meat was at last removed from the shackles of rationing. This was the last item of food to be removed and ration books could now

be discarded. Many people ceremoniously tore up their ration books as a symbolic gesture: normality had at last been achieved.

Deregulation, as suggested, had been gradual. In July 1948 bread was no longer on ration. This may seem rather strange as it wasn't rationed during the war years, but due to a worldwide shortage of grain in 1946, rationing had had to be introduced.

In December 1948 preserves were removed from rationing, but it would be almost another four years before the next item of foodstuffs would be removed. In October 1952 tea was at last taken off the ration book: this prompted a mini celebration as the old British 'cuppa' was part of our heritage. The many tea-growing nations around the world had at last sufficient quantities to supply this country and others.

February 1953 saw sweets taken off ration, thus giving children great delight. The following month the distribution of eggs was no longer controlled, while in April it became possible to obtain cream – impossible to buy during the years of rationing. Another good month for the public was September, when sugar was taken off the ration. At this time people were hoping that meat would be removed from rationing in time for Christmas, but this had to be delayed for a few months: in fact it was the following June before meat was freely available. Butter, margarine, cooking fats and cheese were all taken off ration the previous month, in May and then, following the availability of meat, ration books were no longer required.

The Ministry of Food, so very important during the war years, now had another job. As well as controlling foods and offering advice, it gave a large number of demonstrations to young women who were leaving the services and now cooking for the first time.

In the late 1940s there were sparse supplies of oranges arriving in Britain, and so at last people could make real marmalade rather than a substitute based on apples and carrots.

THE LIGHTER SIDE OF WAR 4

A national newspaper, July 1940.

It's Worth Knowing

Do you know that if you fail to carry your identity card you may be fined anything up to £50 and sent to prison. Police in various parts of the country have already taken proceedings in a number of cases.

An official said,'Persons who do not carry their identity cards might land themselves in serious trouble. Despite warnings, there are many people, — and women seem to be the chief offenders, — who do not appreciate the importance of carrying their identity cards.

Do you know that if you trespass on agricultural land, on which there is a growing crop, other than grass, to look at the damage caused by a bomb, you may be fined £50?

Recently, a bomb dropped on agriculture land but did little damage; sightseers ruined 25 acres of wheat.

Do you know that if you see a barrage balloon drifting near the earth, you should tie its guy ropes to a tree or fence and then inform the police. But you must take precautions. Don't smoke or take naked lights near the balloon; don't touch the cable or other metal parts; don't walk on the fabric or remove any other part of the accompanying gear. Don't touch the red rope, and anchor the balloon by the guy ropes.

THE WAR IN HOVE
including Portslade and Southwick

In June 1940 soldiers were ordered to clear the Brighton and Hove beaches of all bathers – in this (presumably posed) photograph a very young child indeed.

Air Raid Information Centre

In 1940 it was essential to set up a central information centre, a place where local people could make enquiries about relatives and the hospitals where they might have been taken for treatment, together with other information regarding animals and property.

The information centres and hospitals were as follows:

HOVE.
Public Health Department,Town Hall, Church Road
Hove General Hospital
The Lady Chichester Hospital
The Police Seaside Home.

PORTSLADE
Council offices.
Same hospitals as Hove.

SHOREHAM
Shoreham Information Centre.
Southlands Hospital.

SOUTHWICK
Southwick Information Centre.
Southlands Hospital.

Hove's War Years

Although Hove experienced less of an ordeal than her sister town, Brighton, a number of bombs fell on the town and many people lost their lives. Sadly, many wartime records have been destroyed, presenting difficulties in recording exact figures, as the various totals are prone to slight changes. The figures in these pages are believed to be correct, but I take no responsibilities for any mistakes. Many wartime documents have been scanned in compiling the figures, which are believed to be accurate.

There were a total of 1,099 air raid alerts. Some 91 high explosive bombs, three parachute mines and several hundred incendiary bombs were dropped, and there were many attacks involving machine-gunning and canon fire.

The longest recorded air raid alert lasted 13 hours and 40 minutes. This alarm occurred from 6pm on 22nd November 1940 until 7.40am the following morning. The largest number of 'red' warnings (sirens) in one day was eight on 8th October 1940.

The total numbers of civilian people killed as a direct result of the air attacks amounted to 29, while 153 people suffered serious injuries. Added to those numbers were hundreds of people suffering what were officially classed as 'slight' injuries. Many of the casualties sustained appalling injuries, suffering from them for the rest of their lives.

It is recorded that seven servicemen lost their lives while in the borough, but the figure does not include those who died through stepping on mines.

Eighty buildings, mainly houses, were either completely destroyed or had to be demolished due to their dangerous condition. Another 134 were badly damaged, but 129 of these were able to be repaired and made habitable, while some 4,800 properties suffered minor damage.

Hove's worst air attack occurred on Tuesday 9th March 1943 when, around tea-time, four Focke-Wulf 190s fighter-bombers swept in low across the town where they bombed and strafed with their guns. They flew in so low that one of their bombs went through the top of a building in an almost horizontal position before it struck a house and exploded. A dozen people were killed in this raid, with many others badly hurt.

Another air attack later in the same month also caused a large number of casualties including more fatalities and a large number of seriously injured residents.

As a result of these two air attacks, 22 people lost their lives and another 104 people were injured, many seriously. This was a major test for all the civil defence services, especially the rescue and casualty services.

There were some lucky escapes during the war years, and none more so than when four bombs straddled a block of flats causing a few minor injuries but no fatal casualties. Another escape occurred when a bomb hit a printing works: there were 17 members of staff inside, but although some were buried in the debris and among the machinery, no one was killed – mainly due to the prompt and efficient work carried out by the ARP rescue services. There were a few serious injuries among the staff but they all lived to tell the tale.

Hove's First Air Attack, 30th June 1940

Saturday had been one of those summer days that, these days are just dreamed about, sunny all day and very warm. Hove residents had spent the day bathing in the beautiful sun, strolling along the seafront or taking part in a little gardening, tending the vegetable plot that many people were now involved with – all unaware of what fear the night was going to bring them.

The scene was set for the first raid by enemy aircraft on either Hove or Brighton. People went to bed at their normal time and settled down. It was very warm and some were having difficulty

Hove prepares for war. The photograph shows local members of the LDV – forerunner of the Home Guard. (Brighton Local Studies Library)

War Operations Circular
18th October 1940

Where circumstances permit of normal burial and the funeral is carried out by the Local Authority, a grant of £7.10s. will be made to the Local Authority in each case in respect of the cost of the coffin and the conveyance of the body to the cemetery and of fees and charges and other incidental expenses in connection with the burial.

getting to sleep. It was said later that some people had a feeling that something was going to happen. Was it this, and not the warm night, that stopped them enjoying their slumbers?

It was a little after midnight when the sirens began to wail, almost immediately followed by the 'pips'. There was confusion in some houses: was this 'it'? Was this a real air attack on them? While some dithered, others quickly made their way to their shelters or sought refuge under the stairs.

Soon the enemy aircraft engines were clearly heard, although they were not instantly recognised. How could they be? They might be British aircraft the listeners heard. Then came the sounds of explosions as bombs fell, followed by machine gun and canon fire as an aircraft raked the town with its guns.

The raid was soon over, much more quickly than people believed, but the fear was just the same. The children readily admitted that it was all very exciting, something new in their young lives. People were soon out in the streets looking to see what had happened. They had little or no thought for their own safety, forgetting maybe that the aircraft could return.

A single aircraft was responsible, and soon the searchlights were on and searching the night skies for the raider. There was great excitement by the crews of the searchlight as they coned the German aircraft. The guns were soon in action, but the raider managed to extricate himself from the powerful beam and escape into the night sky. Still the AA guns continued firing, without success.

Two small bombs landed close together some distance from the clubhouse at West Hove golf course, making two craters and scorching a few trees in the vicinity. Windows on a housing estate adjoining the golf course were blown in, and the force of the explosions shattered a number of chicken sheds, their occupants being killed. A little further away it was reported that windows and doors shook, and some ornaments fell from their shelves.

The sounds of these bombs exploding could be heard several miles away but still did not arouse some people from their beds. Another bomb, possibly two, fell in Sharpthorne Crescent, Portslade. The blast from these bombs caused some minimal damage but didn't result in either deaths or injuries to the local residents.

A member of the Local Defence Volunteers, who was on duty and not far away from where the two bombs fell on the golf course, said 'I think there must have been two or three machines circling around at the time of the raid. They were at a very great height – probably something like 2,000 feet. It seemed to me that the bombs were meant for the searchlights. They weren't of the 'screaming' type, but they made a loud whistling noise as they descended, offering warning of what was about to happen. After the bombs had been dropped the raiders went away, but they were heard overhead a short while afterwards.'

The local police stood guard over the bomb craters; preventing members of the public collecting souvenirs. All day Sunday people flocked to the region of the golf course, but as it was on private land and there was nothing to see from outside the area, their pilgrimage was in vain.

There were no deaths in this, the first air attack, but three people were treated for minor injuries – cuts from flying glass. These casualties were treated at the scene and did not attend hospital.

The War Price List in 1940

Lord Beaverbrook, the wartime cabinet member, was desperate to raise funds for the war effort. He appealed to everyone to dip into their pockets and donate even the smallest of coins. People in small towns and villages and in clubs and offices couldn't raise very much money, yet they liked to feel that the money they got together was going to buy something definite with which to wallop the Nazis.

Here is a list of approximate prices taken from official sources ranging from £4 (which bought a pistol) to £25,000 (the cost of a heavy bomber):

Pistol	£4
100 rounds of rifle ammunition	£5.10s
Mortar	£40
Machine gun	£100
Percussion mine	£150
16in shell	£150
100 rifles	£700
A small gun	£1,500
A light A.A.gun.	£3,000
A heavy A.A.gun.	£6,000
Fighter plane	£10,000
Heavy bomber	£25,000

July 15th 1940

The night had been punctuated by squally showers, but as daylight appeared the showers turned to fine rain and the day started in a dismal and miserable way.

Hove had already had a taste of the war when the bombs were dropped on the town about two weeks previously. War was something that the town's residents would never get used to, but at this stage it was still very new to them. However, at the sound of the air raid sirens people hurried to whatever shelter they had, praying that they would be spared death or serious injury. The sirens began their wail at 6.14am, and the locals had two minutes to seek shelter before the first of eight small bombs rained down.

Strangely, these bombs all fell quite close to one another in the New Church Road area, causing considerable damage to adjoining streets. It was close to a miracle that more people weren't injured or even killed.

Eric Masters was a coal lorry driver during the first few years of the war before he was called up. He said: 'I got up early to go to work as usual. My mother also got up to make me a cup of tea. I was just leaving when I heard a very loud piercing whistling sound. I looked up and saw a Dornier Do 17 flying southwest some 5,000 feet up, just below the clouds and coming our way. As this was to be our first experience of bombs dropping, we saw no real danger. I said to my mother, "That whistling sound is made by a Spitfire diving on it". How naive of me: we were soon diving back indoors.

'There was a succession of bomb explosions. When we came back out there was no sign of the Dornier, but there were puffs of smoke towards Hove, rising up. I said to my mother, "The b*******! They've started bombing us." For us, that morning, the war had taken an ugly turning for the worse. In fact, it should have come home to us that our peace and quiet was now shattered: a lot more was to come later.

'There were nine 50kg bombs in all, and they fell in a stick across Pembroke Crescent. Some fell in back gardens, but one scored a direct hit on a house in Pembroke Crescent and now sports a very attractive roof of green tiles. Another bomb fell in New Church Road, right on the bus stop outside of St. Christopher's school. The last one landed on the west side pavement about 50 yards from the junction of Westbourne Road.

This aircraft had just dropped around nine bombs 50kg. bombs in Whitehawk, where there was some loss of life.'

On guard at the West Pier. This photograph was taken in April/May 1940. Note the people walking along the seafront. (Brighton Local Studies Library)

13th August 1940

Early on Tuesday morning 13th August 1940, the collier *Betswood* was lying alongside New Wharf in Shoreham Harbour. The captain's orders were to proceed to Portsmouth as soon as the cargo had been discharged, and not to wait for the return of the convoy. The reason was that she was to be better armed than the single old Lewis gun that was their only protection.

The ship was due to sail at 7am, but at 6.30am the sirens sounded and Captain Potts ordered the crew of the Lewis gun to their post. He decided to stay in the confines of the harbour, as this gave him added protection from the local A.A.defences. A few minutes after 7am five German aircraft appeared, flying low and in a line abreast formation. They were coming in from the north of Shoreham and flying out to sea. One of these aircraft still carried a bomb load, and it headed straight for the *Betswood*. The aircraft dropped down to around 500 feet, its engines whining, and then delivered its deadly cargo of bombs.

Five bombs were dropped and thundered into the sea and onto the mud banks at the stern of the ship, somewhere between 70 to 100 yards distant. Captain Potts had been watching the whole incident with some concern, but he told the gun crew to withhold their fire until the very last moment as he didn't want to waste ammunition. The gun crew coolly did as they were instructed, knowing that there wouldn't be time to fix another drum of bullets to the gun.

The gun crew consisted of three of the ship's personnel, namely, Dave Bennett, ordinary seaman Halcrow and the ship's fireman, Patrick. They chose their moment wisely and then let the whole of 50 rounds from the drum off in one mighty stuttering burst. They hit the aircraft: Captain Potts said later that he saw the bullets raking the fuselage. The pilot lost control for a moment as the aircraft took an erratic course, veering violently as it lost height. It narrowly missed a shingle bank and then vanished out over the harbour entrance, flying low, just above the waves.

Some local people on the pier saw it crash into the sea about a mile south of the harbour with a giant splash.

The *Betswood*'s Lewis gun was the only gun firing at that time, and so the credit has to go to the ship's gun crew for downing the enemy aircraft.

However, the collier didn't get away scot free. The five bombs, bursting close astern, had thrown up fountains of seaweed, dirty water and harbour mud, completely covering her – a terrible sight. Captain Potts was furious, using unprintable language because his ship had only recently been painted.

26th August 1940

Monday 26th August started rather cloudy, but it was yet another dry summer's day as Hove residents lay asleep in their beds. A few people were already out on the streets as they made their way to work. Local council staff were enjoying a cup of tea just prior to starting their day's work when the sirens once again warned of impending danger.

It was 5.36am when the first bombs starting falling. The main body of the German bombers was once again targeting RAF airfields, chiefly over Kent and Essex. It was strange that just two enemy bombers had made a beeline for Hove – or, at least, that's how it seemed.

On this occasion it was very fortunate that sufficient warning had been given, allowing plenty of time for the residents to seek shelter. The sound of the bombs exploding was still alien to them, but they nevertheless knew exactly what was happening. Once again there was no panic as they lay or sat in their shelters listening to the Ack Ack guns booming as the shells hurtled skywards in their vain effort to shoot the enemy from the skies.

Stapley Road on 26th August 1940.

In the two air attacks prior to this raid just 11 bombs had been dropped, but now another nine high explosive bombs were falling, and all struck houses in the Stapley Road, Rowan Avenue and Elm Drive area. This caused major damage, and the collapse of several houses buried the occupants in their shelters.

As usual, the air attack lasted no more than about 30 seconds but in that time considerable damage had been caused. The rescue services were still in their infancy in regards to coping with the real thing, although most were very experienced in the practice side of ARP rescue work. They were quickly on the scene in the three main areas of damage. Calls for help were heard in a number of badly damaged houses, and neighbours were quick to be of assistance. This was a good time for the military to be used, and so two units were called in with their vehicles.

In Stapley Road, the rescue workers toiled up to the early part of the afternoon and recovered the body of Mary Munro, an elderly woman of some 87 years. She lived alone in the house, a widow of many years.

Rescue work took place in all the stricken areas and it was almost a miracle that the final toll of the residents was just the one fatality and the sustaining of serious injuries by three other women. There was quite a large number of slightly injured people. Four attended hospital, while some 20 others were treated at the First Aid posts set up by the ARP rescue squads soon after they arrived on the scene.

30th August 1940

Friday 30th August 1940 was one of those wonderful summer days, hot and sunny. Eric Masters, a lorry driver for C.A. Paxton Ltd at Fishersgate, reported for work as usual at about 6.30am, picked up his lorry and set off to Hove goods yard to unload coal from the railway trucks. He then loaded his lorry with coal to take to Brighton and Hove Gas Works, situated on the south side of the harbour at Portslade.

He had made several journeys as the morning progressed, and at about noon he set off with another load of coal. He was driving southwards in Sackville Road, and after passing the junction with Portland Road he noticed that people were running about. He then became acutely aware that his lorry was the only vehicle moving.

He crossed the Church Road junction and saw a police car coming up Hove Street with the public address system booming out and telling people to clear the streets.

'By then,' he said later, 'I was aware of the sounds of aircraft engines overhead. I stopped outside no. 19 Hove Street and knocked on the door. I needed to take cover. A lady opened the door, took one look at me, said "No!" and then shut the door. The problem was that having been at work for some hours moving coal I was as black as the ace of spades. I looked up: the sky was full of Heinkel He 111s flying south-east at about 10,000 feet or more in formation. There were also a number of ME 109s, their protectors: these were involved in a dogfight with some Hurricanes. The sounds of the hurricanes' machine guns and the ME 109s' canon fire were easily identifiable.

'I soon realised that there were no bombs falling, but empty machine gun and canon shell cases were falling down into the streets. I decided that the best place for me was back in the cab of my lorry. I drove off down to the Kingsway and turned westwards. I was driving slowly about 15mph and leaning forward keeping my eye on the sky in case a low flying aircraft appeared. I got as far as Wish Road when suddenly I froze in my seat. I saw a fighter at about 3,000 feet in a dive and coming straight towards me from the south-west out over the lagoon. I started to pull up in order to get out to watch the plane when I noticed that he was slowly turning north away from me. He was in a 45-degree bank away from me and heading inland. I then saw that it was 'one of ours', as they used to say. In fact it was a Hawker Hurricane [no. P3179]. Its carburettor air intake was on fire and flames were licking back under its belly. The propeller was only 'windmilling', and there was hardly a sound from it. It was heading down at about a 45° angle; I just watched it.

'My first impressions were that he was diving out of the battle for safety and that he was going to pull out of the dive low down over the rooftops to escape. I remember thinking to myself that if he didn't soon pull out he would crash. I sat there, and when he passed in front of me he was less than 1,000 feet away. I said to myself, "Pull up, pull up!". But he carried on and ploughed into the ground.

A great mushroom of smoke and flame rose up to about 200 feet. I got out of my cab and my feet and legs just crumbled away from under me. I was very shocked. Just then a policeman, who was on guard at the harbour entrance, shouted at me to get off the road and to take cover. I immediately got back in my lorry and drove about 300 yards to a large shed just to the east of the Adur public house. There was a line of vehicles parked up outside. I stopped and dived into the shed. My boss was already there and told me off for being out on the road. I was 18 years old at this time and, living at this time of great stress, many funny things happened.

'There were some 10 to 15 of us in this large shed huddled together against the back wall. It was semi-derelict and had a large part of the roof missing, which was a slate roof. We felt safe within the thick stone walls. Very soon after I got there the drone of aircraft noises decreased as they flew off back across the sea. Our boss said, "Okay, it's all over," and we went back to work.

I heard that the Hurricane had crashed in the front garden and pavement of no. 49 Woodhouse Road, and so next day I drove that way to take a look. The gable at the top front of the house was all smashed in, and the houses and the east side of Portland Gate flats were completely blackened from the fireball that occurred at the time of the crash.'

The Hurricane crashed at speed and buried itself into the ground with just the tail plane showing. This part of the plane was removed by 32 MU RAF, based at Faygate, near Crawley, while the local council was responsible for repairing damage to the highway.

The pilot of the Hurricane was Sergeant Denis Noble of 43 Squadron, based at Tangmere, and he was just 20-years-old. His commanding officer,. Squadron Leader John Badger, was also shot down later that day during combat over Kent and died from his injuries nine months later.

However, the squadron got their own back when at about 1.20pm on Wednesday 4th September they engaged and shot down a number of Me110s over Sussex as they were returning from a bombing raid.

Two airmen who died on this day: Hurricane pilot Sgt Denis Noble (above) and his commanding officer, Squadron Leader John 'Tubby' Badger (left).

Air Crash, September 9th 1940

Monday 9th September 1940 had been quite a pleasant day and Eric Masters, recounting an incident on this day, remembered that it had also been a quiet day in regards to air activity.

'At about 5.15 pm I left the garage and came home. Just after I arrived, there were the sounds of aircraft buzzing around towards Shoreham, accompanied by canon and machine gun fire. These aircraft were very high, and because of the position of the sun I couldn't pick them out. A minute or two later, looking to the north, I saw a Hurricane in a vertical dive. It crashed on the downs: it went behind the hill for a second and then a pall of smoke came up.

It actually crashed at Saddlescombe Farm, right alongside the Southdown way. The pilot had already baled out over Southwick. I never did find out where he landed, but I believe that he was slightly injured and taken to hospital. During this incident I didn't hear any bombs fall or explode.

Author's note: The pilot was Flight Sergeant Kazimierz Wunsche, RAF No.P2096, of 303 (Polish) Squadron based at Northolt, and the aircraft was Hurricane P3700. He had been involved in combat over Beachy Head with a large number of Bf 109s. He baled out with slight burns, landed near Devils Dyke and was admitted to Hove hospital in Sackville Road.

F/Sgt Wunsche was 21 years old at this time and had joined the Polish air Force at the age of 18. When Germany invaded Poland he was already a pilot, and he shot down one German fighter plane before escaping from his country.

He joined 303 Squadron on its formation in August 1940 and was awarded several medals. He was commissioned in December 1941. He was discharged in 1946 with the rank of Flight Lieutenant, when he returned to Poland. He was credited with the destruction of eight enemy aircraft, (three shared). He died in 1980.

Derek Whatmore's story

These are the memories of a schoolboy, Derek Whatmore, who was bombed out of his home in Portslade on 13th September 1940. It is an extract from his life story, written not commercially but purely for his family and friends.

❲ In September 1940, I was 9 years old and lived with my parents and brother Jim at 25 Fairway Crescent, Portslade. I attended St. Nicholas Junior School in Locks Hill, Portslade, the old flint building near Southern Cross on the Old Shoreham Road. A couple of years later I attended Hove Grammar School. [Now called Blatchington Mill.]

The constant alarm of the air raid sirens and the frequent drone of Dornier and Heinkel aircraft overhead at night resulted in us making up our beds downstairs. Jim slept in the dining room at the back. Mum and Dad had a spare bed in the front room and I slept on the couch, turned to face the middle wall, in the same room.

It was Friday 13th September 1940, some say an unlucky date. We retired to bed, already so used to the sound of aircraft and alarms that we could usually sleep through most of the activities. I was gone in the nothingness of deep sleep, yet suddenly I was leaping over the back of the couch and sprawling head first under my parent's bed, beating them to it by the merest fraction of a second. The room was coming in around our ears. What was happening, happened so quickly that it was only later the sequence of events could be re-lived.

It was hardly a conscious reaction that caused my flight from the couch. There was a shrill whistle of the first, with the second following before the thud of the first bomb. The third was closely followed by the fourth, but by then I had already reached the comparative sanctuary of the floor below the bed. As the fourth bomb of that stick of five landed, the noise was indescribable.

All around, the world seemed to be bursting in upon us,.followed by an eerier quietness except for the settling of lumps of plaster and dust. We scrambled out, Mum and dad with their torches trying to locate the extent of the damage. Mum cut her knee on the glass on the floor as she got up. Dad was already at the front door finding that it was forced inwards and that there was no way out, that way.

He exited by the back door and, skirting the side of the house, flashed his light on a round shaft a mere foot from the concrete path by the front door. He shone the torch down into the depths and saw the different bands of strata of earth, chalk and clay like a geological section. He hurried back to tell us to get out without delay. Despite the blast that had knocked in the front of the house, the bomb on our doorstep had not finished with us yet. Who could say when if it would explode?

Mrs. Fiest, who lived next door, was hanging out of her back bedroom window, enquiring what was going on. An ARP warden came hurrying up to recommend immediate evacuation. We left with no time to collect any of our belongings. We crunched our way through the dust, plaster and broken crockery covering the kitchen floor. The entire contents of the larder had been shot out into the kitchen. Everything was smashed except, miraculously, two eggs in a china bowl which had come to rest in the middle of the floor.

As we scuttled along the road, the Civil Defence men were already throwing a cordon around the end of the road. Renewed cracking of Anti-Aircraft guns and the rumbling thud of dozens of incendiary bombs falling not too far away accompanied us up the hill to a rest centre that had been set up by the Civil Defence in an office opposite the nearby shops We had hardly arrived before I was thrust unceremoniously to the ground, my head under a chair, as another cluster of incendiary bombs made the whole building tremble. Shortly afterwards we were heading back down the hill again and I was tucked up under the eiderdown of Mrs. Piper, my piano teacher. Her house was right at the intersection with our road, about 100 yards away from our house.

Side and front views of no. 25 Fairview Crescent, damaged by a bomb during the night of 13th/14th September, 1940. (Photos D. Whatmore).

The commotion had started about 11.40pm and just before 2am there was a mighty 'whoosh', and Dad was just in time to see a huge mass of chalk descending from a great height, right where our house was supposed to be.

I must have dozed off in Mrs. Piper's house for the rest of the night, but I was up very early the next morning, which was bright and sunny. Little groups were passing and standing around, looking at the damage to our house that by this time had been roped off. The Civil Defence was very much in evidence, clambering amongst the debris of our house and Mrs. Fiest's next door, and holding back unauthorised people from going too close.

There was little left of the roof and front windows, the latter hanging been forced inwards and one of which was hanging precariously by one side. The sidewall was partially collapsed and the remainder was being demolished to make it safe. It was strange how the glass in the window frames upstairs in front was still intact despite the crazy angle at which they had settled. The criss-cross of the sticky paper, which was the fashion of the day to reduce the danger of flying glass, certainly had been effective.

The high bank of the front garden was virtually one large crater, the chalk from which had erupted upwards and had descended on to the roof of our house. Tons of wet chalk had landed on the bed in the front bedroom, forcing the iron legs through the ceiling of the floor below. How lucky we had been to move to the comparative safety of the lower floor. The concrete steps leading down the bank to the front door had all but disappeared except for the large top step with a twisted section of the handrail attached, hanging on the edge of the crater.

Neighbours from all around came to chat, look and discuss, and I began to feel that overnight we had become the centre of attraction. The shed, by the side of the house lacked its roof, but although not even our family were allowed near initially, my little bike was rescued undamaged and I was able to happily follow events with at least one of my treasured possessions intact. Not many of our possessions came out of our ruined home. What could be dug out and rescued was loaded onto an open Corporation lorry, most of it rather the worse for the experience and covered in chalk. The lorry trundled off in search of an empty house with the family, neighbours, curious observers, assorted dogs and me on my bicycle following closely behind.

Tom, our cat appeared: no one knew where he had been. There had been no sight of him during the night and we were all very pleased to see him. The feeling was clearly mutual. I wondered just how many of his nine lives he had lost.

The first stop was an empty house in Mill Lane, but an unexploded bomb (number six) that had not been accounted for was found just over the wall in Goatcher's field. The cavalcade was waved away as the bomb disposal squad arrived, and we returned to Fairway Crescent. No. 57 was empty, and the unloading of the lorry began. Shortly after our arrival the owner of the house appeared with a rent book in his hand. This gesture upset my parents, and they were determined not to stay there any longer than was necessary.

As our few sticks of furniture were unloaded, the army bomb disposal unit was rounding up the UXBs. Three defused bombs, one large and two smaller, lay on display on the back of their truck. One, a 1,000 pounder, had been dug from a garden in Helena Close, hardly fifty yards from our home, while one of the others came from Mill Lane. A bomb had exploded on impact on the allotments close to the Bofors gun site in front of the shops and had succeeded in blowing out a few windows and mutilating a few hundred cabbages. We really had very little left of our furniture and possessions.

One bit of damage that left me with a secret feeling of relief was to the piano. Outwardly, it looked free of serious damage, but when the top was opened, it was found to be choked solid with wet chalk and it was a complete write-off. At least that was the end of my career as a budding concert pianist. I had always struggled to find time to practice and could never raise the enthusiasm, and certainly not the talent, that Mum would have liked. I think that she was secretly hoping I would have fulfilled her own aspiration.

In weeks to come, a government assessor inspected the remains and made light of our losses. We were eventually awarded the princely sum of £21 as compensation. This amount was supposed to re-furnish our home. Within a month we managed to leave the rented house at no. 57 and move two doors away to no. 61. We still had to pay rent, but the arrangements were happier. After the war our old house was re-built and we moved back, but in the meantime my parents had paid several hundreds of pounds in rent and there was no compensation for that.

Nevertheless, we counted ourselves lucky to have survived at all when compared with the scale of death, grief and destruction suffered by so many thousands elsewhere.)

14th September 1940

Just over a year had now passed since the start of the war and Hove residents hadn't been troubled too much in the first year. They had suffered only four air attacks, and although two people had been killed and 11 people had sustained serious injuries, it could have been a lot worse. They were certainly affected by rationing, and of course they were seeing the variety of food available gradually diminishing. They had opened their homes to a large number of children who had been evacuated from the London area. They had also witnessed many dogfights overhead during the Battle of Britain, which was about to reach its climax.

At about 1.30am on Saturday 14th September they were awakened by the wail of the sirens and quickly made their way to their air raid shelters. A few minutes later enemy aircraft were above and dropped somewhere around 65 incendiary bombs, following up with an oil bomb. Most of these small incendiary bombs weighed about two pounds each. They fell in the same area as the previous air attack on the town in the Egmont Road. The bombs scattered across nearby streets, causing small roof fires, but these were quickly extinguished and the only damage caused was to two unoccupied houses near the end of the street. A number of these incendiary bombs fell in the nearby cemetery, causing no damage. The oil bomb also fell in the cemetery and caused slight damage to a few headstones.

Come the afternoon the enemy aircraft returned, and this time the raid was a lot more serious with high explosive bombs being dropped. It was just after 3.30pm when the wail of the sirens gave notice of an imminent attack. A few people appeared to ignore the danger and carried on with their tasks, while others hurried to whatever shelter was available. About five minutes later the aircraft could be heard, and people in the home shelters braced themselves. There was something different about a daylight raid compared with one at night: it didn't seem quite so frightening and yet, as always, there was the fear of the unknown.

It appeared that there were just two aircraft, and soon the bombs could be heard exploding right across the town. They fell in the same area, with one hitting homes in Salisbury Road, while others hit dwelling houses in other streets including Grand Avenue and Eaton Road. One bomb failed to go off, making a total of six. The aircraft quickly made off back across the Channel and although the local guns attempted to shoot them down, they probably made it safely home to France.

The rescue services were on the scene in minutes, being deployed at all the bombed sites. Many houses suffered very serious damage, with some being almost fully demolished due to the danger that they could cause to the rescuers. Several people were buried beneath the ruins of their homes. A number of soldiers were summoned and performed valiant service. One by one the injured people were rescued from their homes and taken by ambulance to the hospital. One couple buried in the ruins of their home were not released for many hours and were then rushed to hospital, where their condition was reported to be 'satisfactory': they did go on to make a full recovery. Three other people were treated at hospital but were not detained, while the first aid parties of the rescue services treated about ten people, including two children.

The unexploded bomb gave the authorities a great problem, as many people had to be evacuated from their homes and put up in a local church hall. The police had to arrange a diversion, and officers spent hours on traffic duty while several others stood nearby keeping inquisitive people away.

There was a dreadfule finale. On Tuesday the 24th September a group of soldiers was working on the unexploded bomb, still *in situ*, to make it safe when it suddenly exploded. Three of them were killed instantly, and the explosion caused very serious damage to properties over a large area.

Eric Masters' Narrow Escape

This is a wartime story as written by Eric Masters, who in the early part of the war was a coal lorry driver moving coal to the gasworks.

❬ It dawned a fairly nice day on September 26th 1940 and I found that for that day I was back on the Kingston Wharf coal run. By now the gas works sports area was full of coal, the paint shop was virtually surrounded and rail borne supplies were dropping off. The facilities at Kingston Wharf had been extended, and so the use of Hove goods yard was greatly reduced. A further development in coal movement was that, with the hours of darkness increasing and with better protection, more colliers were now getting through the Channel, so reducing the need for rail deliveries.

It had been a quiet day, and by 4pm I was loaded with my 15th load. (That was regarded as a day's work and paid three shillings bonus on top of my wages.) All the drivers were now in the little teashop under the long demolished road bridge over the railway line to the wharf. There was no air raid on and I heard an aeroplane, which I didn't like the sound of. We dashed out of the teashop and saw a Junkers Ju 88 about 3/4,000 feet up and turning towards the south-west. It went into a dive. I saw four bombs falling from it, and a few seconds later saw the resulting pillars of smoke and debris thrown up in the air in the direction of Shoreham town centre when they struck.

Dickie Colborn, another driver who was particularly touchy with the bombing, shouted out "I'm not stopping here, I'm off!" and he started a bit of a stampede to get off the wharf. Had I known what I was letting myself in for I would have sat tight. We trailed off to the works to unload our coal, but when we got there, we found that there was a 'warning on' as the gates were shut.

Ever since July when the warnings had first started sounding, the gas works had had a practice of shutting all the gates and denying exit or admission to anyone. When I arrived there was quite a queue of lorries, and I was almost stopped under the two large cranes used to unload the ships. I got out and wandered up to the lorry just in front of me and started to talk with the driver. We were discussing the Shoreham raid that had just occurred when all of a sudden there was the roar of aircraft engines being opened up and I turned around and saw a Junkers Ju 88 swinging around from the west and heading straight for us in a shallow dive with its machine guns blazing. There I was on the wrong side of the lorry on the open quay and with no shelter.

There was a solid brick wall behind the lorry, but I was far too late to do anything about it. The German bomber was about 300 yards away when it flattened out and dropped four bombs, and for a moment I took my eye off him. I just watched these bombs go sailing over, about 250 feet up in front of me, and disappear over No. 1 and No. 2 retort houses. I have no recollection of any noise, just a trembling of the ground and a violent rush through the gap of the retort houses and a billowing cloud of burning gas going up 300 feet or more in the air. In this mass of gas and debris were hundreds of wooden planks, 6ft.x 1ft x 1 inch thick. This was the coal shed's roof that covered about 1 acre, going up as well. At this stage, I made a beeline for my lorry, crawled underneath it and waited for that lot to come down. I suppose from start to finish it was all over in about 20 seconds.

About 20 minutes later, while on the sports field unloading, I saw another Junkers Ju 88 going out seawards to the west over Southwick and trailing smoke. The aircraft had its nose down and was gradually losing height. I remember saying to myself, "I hope you don't make it you b*******!" I watched it until it disappeared, and unfortunately he was still flying. ❯

Author's note: It was reported that one Junkers Ju 88 crash-landed at Evreux airfield due to damage caused over southern England. Was it the one trailing smoke that Eric Masters saw?

8th October 1940
Portslade

Eric Masters has an incredible number of local wartime stories covering the period from the very start of hostilities through to about the middle of 1942 when it was his turn to be called up. He has spent a very long time researching the subject of the various air attacks on Hove and Portslade, and I am very grateful to him as he has freely allowed me the benefit of his experience to share with my readers. His name and stories frequently appear in accounts of Hove incidents in the early part of the war.

Tuesday October 8th 1940 started very cloudy but with quite a strong wind blowing – not the type of weather suitable for an air attack. However, inland the cloud base was much higher and visibility much better, and that could be construed as being air raid weather. There were widespread attacks on London, with hundreds of German aircraft taking the usual route over Kent from Dymchurch. In the morning, two formations consisting of 50 and 100 bombers with their escorts, approached London via Kenley and Biggin Hill at 8.30am

Among the targets hit by falling bombs were Charing Cross underground station, Horse Guards Parade, Tower Bridge and the BBC's Bush House. Another attack occurred at about 9.30am and a further one some three hours later. Fighter Command scrambled 639 sorties and lost four of their aircraft, while the enemy lost 14 aircraft.

Eric Masters, at home in Portslade, reports that the day was very quiet until around 7pm. At this time he and the family were out in their large garden. His house was at the end of the road, and they had an excellent view up and down Manor Hall Road, Southwick.

'We started to hear the roar of planes coming in from the southeast and then saw three Heinkel He 111s. They were low-flying, coming in over the roof tops less than 1,000 feet and turning parallel to the railway line going west. All their machine guns were blazing away. With the daylight beginning to fade, you could see by the tracer bullets that they were firing anywhere. One of these bullets went straight through the plate glass window of the hairdressers shop on the corner of Shelldale Avenue and Trafalgar Road, Portslade. The bullets hit the large mirror on the wall and drilled neat holes in it.

As they came by we dived back into our house to escape a chance hit. When we came back out they were turning as if to go back out to sea, when all off a sudden the bombs they had dropped started to detonate. I counted over 40 explosions. The first bombs fell in Kingston Lane, Southwick and destroyed several old cottages on the west side. They also caused severe damage to the then new bungalows in Rectory Gardens, behind a hedge on the east side of the lane. All the others fell in the fields that were then in between Kingston Lane and Stoney Lane. Some ceilings were brought down and some walls were cracked in the new council-owned houses in King George V Road.'

There were a number of casualties in this air attack, some serious, and the victims were conveyed to Southland's Hospital, where they all recovered. One person was killed in her home: 35-year-old Alice Ford of Tile Cottage, Old Rectory Gardens, Kingston Lane, Southwick.

7th November 1940
Hove

More than two weeks had elapsed since the last air attack on Hove.

'It was a funny situation during this time,' recalls Mrs Janet Argyle. 'The night attacks were strangely worse, probably because of the dark, but it was very unnerving. When you had had a night attack like the one towards the end of October, you believed that there would be another one the following night. When it didn't happen then you thought it would come the following night and so on. This really did break your sleep pattern as you went to bed really worried about what might happen. I suppose we had been very lucky, as we had only had about a dozen air raids all year. Really, compared to London, those poor people there, it must have been terrible.

'About 8.15pm on Friday 7th November, the sirens sounded and as usual we hurried to our shelter, downstairs. I remember that it was quite misty, just sea mist though. I heard the German plane and the guns were firing. I hoped that they would shoot it down. I waited in the shelter for the sounds of the bomb, but nothing happened. We were in the shelter for about half an hour before the All Clear sounded. We had been there all that time and nothing had happened.

'This air attack produced the sum of just two incendiary bombs. One fell on a house in Cromwell Road, causing a small roof fire. This was quickly extinguished and there was no damage. However, there was one casualty from this incident. The householder, in his haste to climb his ladder to put the fire out, slipped and injured his left arm. His wife, although worried at the time, later saw the funny side of his fall. The other incendiary bomb fell on a house in St. Johns Road but caused no damage.

'It seems very strange to have an air attack and drop just two incendiary bombs, but it was believed at the time that the aircraft was returning from a bombing raid and, finding that they still had the bombs on board, decided to drop them on British soil before they crossed the Channel and back to base. I suppose it makes sense!'

THE LIGHTER SIDE OF WAR 5

German Airmen

A German pilot, evidently very thirsty, came down with a rush somewhere in south-east England. He threw up his arms when he saw some farm workers and shouted, in a language everyone understood, 'What about a pint of beer?' He was promptly marched off to the local pub.

P.S. The toast was 'England'.

After one of the crew of a Junkers Ju 88 had been captured, he said to his guard, 'I had to get rid of a bomb in a hurry. I hope it didn't hurt anyone.'

The Story of a Garden Pest

A warden sent to examine damage done by falling cannon shells, laboriously complied his official report: 'Damage caused to one vegetable marrow and three runner beans.'

His Chief wasn't too impressed.

Blind Fury

Frederick Head, 25 years, of Addington Surrey, tampered with a derelict car placed in a field on the instructions of the Air Ministry, and was fined £1. His plea of guilty was accepted.

The prosecution stated that he took the blinds from the car to use for his blackouts. In court it was stated that the car, together with others, had been put in the field to prevent the landing of enemy aircraft.

18th November 1940
Portslade

At about 5pm on Saturday 18th November 1940 Eric Masters had arranged to meet his girl friend at her home in Gladstone Road, Portslade. Their intention was to visit the cinema. The weather was dark and dismal, with a solid cloud base only a few thousand feet up.

They were ambling along Gladstone Road, talking about a variety of subjects as they came to mind. Just before they reached the bottom of the road they were alerted by the sound of an aircraft. This aircraft suddenly emerged out of the clouds flying north-west and turning to head to the west. Eric recognised it straight away as being a Heinkel He111. All of its machine guns opened up, spraying bullets everywhere: you could tell by the tracer bullets that they weren't aiming at anything in particular. The idea of almost all air attacks was to frighten people who happened to be in the streets at the time – and there was no doubt on this occasions that they achieved their object.

'I didn't see or hear the German bomber release its bombs. This must have happened before the aircraft came into my view. However, we both dived in the doorway of a house. Luckily we were on the south side of the road, and we were protected by the house from any wayward bullets. We did hear about nine bomb explosions somewhere to the south of us but didn't know exactly where they had fallen. Once again, it was all over in seconds, the plane went away and after we got over the sudden shock we came out on to the pavement and carried on our way.

'When I got to work on the Monday morning I learnt that a ship had been struck by the last of the stick of nine bombs and it had hit the galley at the stern. It killed a young butcher's boy who was delivering meat to the ship. Had the German bomb aimer held the release for just a few seconds more his bombs would have fallen right across the large petrol storage tanks the ship was unloading into. Had that happened, and had that amount of petrol ignited, Portslade would have had a massive fire on its hands.

'Later that morning I was tipping a load of coal under the west crane when I noticed a large gouge in the concrete about six feet long and pointing towards the petrol installation on the other side of the canal. It was first thought that all the bombs that missed the ship had fallen into the canal, but apparently the first one struck the concrete quay on the south side, skidded along it and went into the water.

'The ship was the tanker *Shellbrit II*, and she was lying alongside what was at the time the Regent Oil Wharf, situated opposite the bottom of Church Road, Portslade. It's now a concrete batching plant.

The *Shellbrit II* was later moved down into Aldrington Basin where Streeter's, the local ship repairers, renovated it. She left harbour, fully repaired, in the spring of 1941.'

Author's note: The butcher's boy killed was 17-year-old William Wood, the son of Mr. And Mrs. Sidney Wood of 118, Southwick Street, Southwick.

St Michael's & All Angels Church Southwick

The church of Saint Michael and all Angels, Southwick boasts an 11th century tower. The chancel and the south arcade are of about the same period, with inserted windows of the 13th century in the north wall. The remainder of the church, in particular the knave and aisles, were rebuilt, in a very debased style, in 1834, the vestry and organ chamber following in 1893. All in all it is a fine church, steeped in history.

During the latter part of February 1941 the tower of the church was badly damaged by a bomb dropped by enemy aircraft during a raid on Southwick. It was a dismal Friday afternoon, the 21st February, when the Bishop of Chichester, Dr. Bell, inspected the damage. The tower had been scarred with cracks from top to bottom, and it was feared that the church might have to demolished.

The bomb disposal unit, under the direction of Col. Sydney Lynn, was consulted, because the bomb had buried itself deep in the foundations. The problem at this stage was that it was unknown whether the bomb was was

The church showing huge cracks after the bombing raid.

Each stone was numbered and used in order when the church was rebuilt.

harbouring a time delay and was therefore likely to explode should it be disturbed.

After careful examination, a large deep hole was excavated where the course of the bomb was detected – yet, strangely, no bomb was found. The hole was filled and a second excavation took place just north of the first excavation, when again a bomb track was found. Again, no bomb was discovered. This then was a very worrying time for the unit: they knew that there was a bomb, but where?

The tower was now in a very precarious condition, due first to the damage caused by the bomb and the dislocation of the soil by its impact, and secondly to the two large excavations made by the bomb disposal unit. Since it was obvious that they couldn't risk yet another large excavation trying to find the bomb, Col Lynn refused to undertake any further work until the tower had been demolished.

The Ancient Monuments department of the Ministry of Works arrived to inspect the situation. Long discussions took place and numerous suggestions were investigated in the vain hope that the damaged historical tower would not have to be demolished – such a drastic measure for the church and its congregation, with many prayers no doubt being offered up. These discussions continued for many days, until it was ultimately decided by all concerned that there was no other safe course. The tower would be taken down, with all the pieces carefully marked, and would be reconstructed as soon as it was expedient to do so.

Scaffolding was erected around the tower, and all the stones and pieces of timber, which had previously been numbered and recorded on drawings, were collected together with the old flints in a corner of the churchyard and stored under corrugated iron for about seven years. The stones were numbered from the top of each angle quoin on each face of the tower, beginning with no.1 and continuing stone by stone down to ground level. Needless to say, this was an incredible feat, but the time taken in preparation was used to good effect – as was proved when the tower was rebuilt. During the interval between the demolition and the rebuilding, the west end of the church was supported on temporary shoring, careful watch being kept to see that there was no movement.

When the tower had been taken down, it was first suggested that the bomb might be better left alone, but the disposal unit returned and eventually undertook a third excavation beneath the famous old church.

This time it met with success: a massive one-ton bomb was discovered near the west end of the north aisle of the church on New Year's Day 1943, having been embedded beneath the church for close on two years. It had dived down to a depth of some thirty feet and then taken a strange upward course. It was defused and removed.

Author's note: During the night of the 21st February 1941 a second bomb fell and exploded to the south of the church. This caused considerable damage to local housing but not to the church.

The above story is based on *The Tower and Spire of the Church of Saint Michael and All Angels,* the account of the demolition and rebuilding subsequent to damage sustained during the Second World War, by John L. Denman F.S.A.

Parachute Mine
Nevill Road, 28th April 1941

Here are two accounts of a parachute mine explosion which slightly injured three men and seven women, with one male serviceman being taken to hospital.

The first account is taken from the diary of George Horrobin, then living in Court Farm Road:

George Horrobin

'It was grandfather's birthday and at about 10.15pm Rosie was in the kitchen and Dad, Mum and I were in the front room. Then 'Bang, tinkle tinkle'! Mum rushed to the kitchen to Rosie. I tried to open the kitchen door but it was jammed. I thought she was holding it the other side, but she was calling for Dad. I charged the door and then went up to Grandfather. He had got up and was about to come down. Dad went to open the front door but it had blown open and the lock was on the floor. Dad propped it shut with a stick. We then all got our coats on and went outside to have a look. Some neighbours, Mr and Mrs Parsons, were examining their front porch. Lights were shining everywhere through the remains of the blackout curtains and doors.

'Mum and I went up Court Farm Road to look. We were met by Mr.Chatt: he had got it badly. Just then the All Clear sounded. We went around the corner to no. 191 Nevill Road and saw the rescue workers and the damage. Then Mollie and Mrs Spiess arrived and Mum and Dad went back with them.

'About 3.30am, just as we were getting settled, there was somebody knocking at the door. Mum got up and let them in. They were the Spiess family, and they had been evacuated with the rest of the Holmes Avenue people because of the bomb. Mum and I got up about 6am and went around to view the damage. We saw the hole and picked up bits of the mine, and I found a bit of the parachute cord by the hole.'

Landmine blast at no. 197 Nevill Road, Hove.

The second account is from Doris Shoulders, who was 21 years old and living with her sister at 151 Nevill Avenue. She clearly remembers the very loud sounds of a bomb exploding somewhere in the Fallowfield Crescent area. Following this, a landmine fell in Nevill Avenue but failed to explode. This mine's fall had been blocked when it became wedged between an apple tree and a lean-to garden shed. The police and ARP Services arrived quickly on the scene and ordered everyone to leave their homes and go to the nearby Bishop Hannington's church hall in Holmes Avenue.

'There were crowds of us packing into the hall' she said, 'and soon afterwards we were getting settled down for the night. At about 1am the authorities had a change of mind and decided we were still a little too near the unexploded German mine for safety, and so a number of buses arrived and we were moved to a church hall in Tamworth Road. Some of us managed to get some sleep.

'In the morning we were given a cup of tea and breakfast: this consisted of rolls, jam, butter and a cup of tea. At about 6.30 – 7 many people set off for work.

'The Army Disposal Unit from Portsmouth dismantled the mine during the morning and we were allowed to return to our homes in the early afternoon.'

14th June 1941

Mary Priest, who was just 15 years old, attended Hove County School for girls in Nevill Road. She lived with her parents at 65 Western Road Hove. She was a very popular girl, with many friends. She enjoyed school and could be described as a model pupil.

On Friday 13th June 1941 she said goodbye to her classmates and caught a bus with a couple of her friends who also lived in the Western Road area. Mary's home was close to Holland Road, while her friends lived in one of the nearby streets.

She visited one of these friends in the evening after she had had her meal and had completed her homework. Her mother was very strict regarding her homework, feeling that it was so important to her

Debris being cleared in the Western Street, Hove, area after bombs fell on 14th June 1941. (J. Seville, Hove)

general schoolwork. Her mother didn't mind her going out, but insisted that she took proper precautions during any air raid and also insisted that she should not be out late into the evening.

She heeded her mother, coming home quite early, and was looking forward to the following day when she had arranged to go shopping in Brighton with her friends.

She went to bed and was asleep as the first hint of trouble arrived. About 2.15am the wail of the sirens was heard, with the pips following almost immediately. There was no time to seek shelter. Her mother called out twice to Mary, the second time just as six H.E. bombs were dropped from an enemy aircraft in an almost straight line, the bomber flying in a south-easterly direction. Two of the bombs fell in the sea

Shops near Palmeira Stores after the bombing raid.

while the other four were destined to fall on shops and dwellings in Hove. One of them fell on 65 Western Road, on the northern side, the building being a shop with accommodation above. Mary was sleeping at the top of the building and therefore had no time to leave her room. The building collapsed and Mary and her parents were buried in the rubble.

Another bomb fell close to a seafront hotel, but with no casualties as the hotel had been evacuated a few days prior to the bomb falling and the new occupants had not yet moved in. This property had

The First Avenue Hotel in Queen's Gardens, badly damaged by a bomb on 14th June 1941.

been earmarked for military occupation. A third bomb struck the roadway in the nearby vicinity and although some dwellings suffered blast damage there were no reported casualties.

The fourth bomb fell in a back street near the seafront hotel, causing damage to garages and lock-ups, while a number of houses suffered damage to their roofs and windows, the main structure of these premises remained undamaged.

Meanwhile the various branches of the rescue workers descended on the collapsed buildings in Western Road and the rubble was soon being removed. The rescue went on for many hours. The first body to be found was Mary's, but she was already dead. Her parents were later rescued, her mother, Dinah, suffering a severe head wound, her father, Frank, just a few scratches and bruises. They were taken to the Hove hospital where they were treated and discharged.

The funeral took place on the 19th June, and Mary was buried in Hove Cemetery. Several local dignitaries attended the funeral, including the mayor, Councillor A. Clarke, the headmistress of Hove County School for Girls, Miss Richards, and representatives of several local organisations.

Soon after this bombing incident a Heinkel He 111 of 3/KGr 100 was intercepted by a Beaufighter and shot down into the sea off Hove seafront. This aircraft may have been responsible for the bombing. The aircraft sank soon after hitting the water, and all the crew died.

A POW's DIARY

Laurence Seale

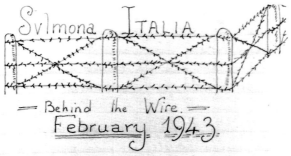

Sulmona ITALIA

= Behind the Wire. =

February 1943.

Good news on the Isr. When parcels arrive. We go one per man, per week again. We have been on half & sometimes quarter issue. On the 7th a batch of parcels arrived. More are expected. Half issue, so far. By 16th a few more parcels arrived. Still half issue. No private parcels, for me yet News still good. The weather still holds fine and warm. The moon shines as brightly, as on the desert. Today is the 21st Sad news. Edies' father died, on 24th Jan.

The German Army captured Private 6097221 Laurence Frank Seale of The Royal Signals Corp on 29th June 1942 in the Western Desert at Mersa Matruh, Egypt. After his capture he decided to write down on scraps of paper what happened in the prisoner-of-war camps.

In general the diary is light on detail. He was at first imprisoned in Italy, and when eventually he arrived in Germany the odd scraps of paper were more or less non-existent. At this camp his POW number was 253135, imprinted on a metal disc which was worn at all times.

The diary is very interesting and gives some insight into the conditions endured by the POWs during World War II. The words strongly portray his emotions of anger, love and fear as the weeks, months and years go by, together with the frustrations of not being able to contact his loved ones.

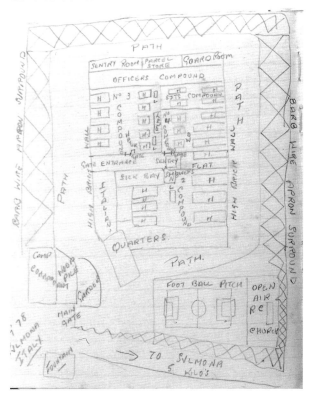

By the end of the war, the scraps of paper were very tattered, and so the contents were written down, together with sketches, in a small hardback book. Those entries have been faithfully copied here. The first page contains Laurence's sketch drawing (*left*) of his first POW camp, situated in Italy about 5 kilometres from Sulmona, a town to the south-east of Rome.

Laurence Seale was captured days after the Allied defeat at Tobruk.

Foreword: Captured, on the disastrous retreat on the Western Desert, in June 1942. I was transferred by stages, via Tobruk, Derna and Benghazi to Italy. Landing at Taranto in July 1942. In this country I was 'mucked about' until I finally settled in PG 78 Sulmona. Until Christmas 1942 I had no means of recording any of my movements. A representative of the Pope gave us diaries in which I wrote the first year of my POW life. The break in the record of my German diary was also the result of the lack of writing materials.

January 1943. Another year, what has it in store for me? I can only hope that freedom and re-union with Edie [his wife] will be mine before 1944. Only enough [food] parcels to last until the 17th of this month. Not so good. I hope some more arrive soon. No parcels up to the 24th. The news and the weather are good. That's something. Received my ninth letter from home on 21st. Tripoli reported in our hands on the 24th. Committed to memory – Chocolate Spread for Civvy Street. Rumours of parcels on the 29th. The sun still shines

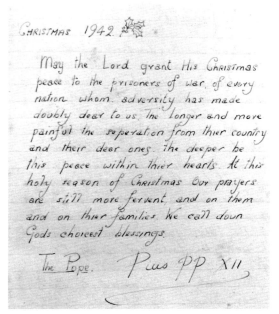

CHRISTMAS 1942.

May the Lord grant His Christmas peace to the prisoners of war, of every nation whom adversity has made doubly dear to us. The longer and more painful the seperation from thier country and their dear ones. the deeper be this peace within thier hearts. At this holy season of Christmas Our prayers are still more fervent, and on them and on thier families. We call down Gods choicest blessings.

The Pope.   Pius PP XII

Pope Pious XII's Christmas message to all prisoners of war, 1942.

bright and warm. The chaps are sunbathing today, the 31st – so another month drags by.

February 1943. Headed 'behind the wire' (With drawing) – Good news on the 1st when parcels arrive. We go one per man, per week again. We have been on half and sometimes quarter issue. On the 7th a batch of parcels arrived; more are expected. Half issue so far. By 16th a few more parcels arrived but still half issue. No private parcels for me yet. News still good, the weather still holds fine and warm. The moon shines as brightly as in the desert. Today is the 21st, sad news, – Edie's father died on 24th January. On the 27th I received a letter from Grace [sister-in law]. Total now 20. A full issue of parcels next week, starting a new month.

March 1943. 'The brew up' with a small drawing. – A good start, the first three weeks have been a full issue of parcels. Also on the 17th I had my first cigarette parcel from home. The news is fair, the weather indifferent, not so much sun, but warm. Letters are slow, only two so far and it's the 19th today. Half the month has gone again. Mail total now 23 including the parcel. Toward the end of the month I heard that Brighton had been bombed. Pray God, that Edie and all are safe. Mail has been very slow indeed. I have had three letters all told this month – four now, the 31st.

Laurence Seale (seated) with two army friends in 1941.

April 1943. Mail has been better this month, 7 letters and 3 parcels. The weather has been very warm. Easter Monday saw the annual pilgrimage, to the monastery in the mountains. The news is not bad either. Started making a table, wonder if I shall finish it. Had our sheets and pillows taken from us. I had a nice wool palliase, which has now been replaced with a straw one, not so soft. Parcel issue has been good, only one week in which we had a half issue.

May 1943. Still no signs of the end yet. Tunisia fell on the 8th of the month. I had 15 communications from home making a total of 51, among them two cigarette parcels. Ron's letter arrived at last. The weather has been changeable, mostly dull and wet during the last week. Let's hope another birthday will not be spent here. We finished our table of tins; it took about 90 tins all told. Playing cricket a bit more now, makes a bit of fun. Good shows – George and Margaret and El Cantina Del Sol. 'Roll on Freedom.'

June 1943. Mail's slow this month. Two islands in the Med. fell early on, arousing some hope of a beginning of the end. Half another year gone by. A good band concert played by our mandoliers, the best band I have heard here. Saturday nights are now record nights. The gramophone is played in the compound. This makes a pleasant change. Fruit is coming in; some peaches have come into the camp. The news of the outside world is scanty but not so bad. Wonder what next month brings.

July 1943. Quite an exciting month. On the 10th we invaded Sicily and got along quite well. Then the Government of Italy was changed and we have high hopes of a peace agreement: I wonder. The newspapers have been stopped, so we are without news, officially. My mail has been slow. I had a cigarette parcel from the Signal Association – 120 State Express cigarettes. The 'duff gen' is terrible these days. The only thing to do is wait and hope for the best. I look eagerly towards next month.

August 1943. Sicily taken by the Allies, since then we have had many air raid alarms. Parcels are short and I see no prospects of any more arriving. Tighten the old belt again. On the 27th Sulmona was bombed (about 5 miles or so from us). About 100 planes came over. Our bungalows shook and rattled. We were without running water and lights for two or three days afterwards. We could see the bombs exploding; the pall of dust was huge. And so to another month of POW life.

September 1943. On the 3rd Sulmona was again bombed, 36 planes this time. Italy invaded, and we hope again. On the 8th Armistice signed, the camp is open now. We wander where we please, inside the outside wire. Alarms though, the Germans retreating. What a change here. On the 12th we took to the hills. After 3 days practically waterless, Jerry recaptured us (15th.). On Friday 17th he put us on a train, all locked in. – Five days and six nights –.On the 22nd we arrived at a Russian camp, waiting to be sent to a 'Stalag camp' near Muisberg on the Elbe. Here conditions were terrible – lice abundant. Hopes dashed.

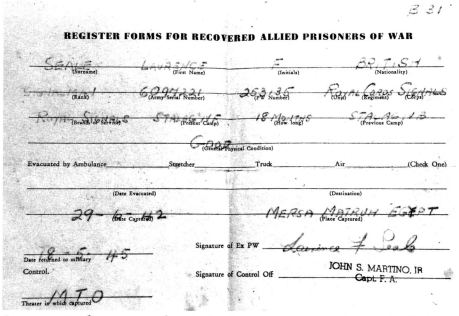

Laurence Seale's 'register form' after he was repatriated from the POW camp in Germany.

October 1943. On the 19th we arrived at IVB Stalag. Here we were disinfested, hair off, vaccinated, inoculated and registered POWs in Germany. We were put into working groups and on the 25th we arrived in Freiberg, Saxony, 206 strong. We commenced work on Wednesday 27th. We are now in Saxony, some are down a mine, some on top. I am on top at present. We have no Red Cross parcels here but hope to see some soon. No writing home yet either. Cards etc. are promised. I wonder how Edie is? When shall I see her again? We had a protest meeting on the 31st – no good though.

November 1943. Month opened lively. Jerry said we were shirking and cut our bread ration down. On the 3rd we stopped work in protest – no effect. Still no cigarettes or parcels. I am navvying in a pit (not mine pit.) We are now on short rations, punishment for strike. Still working on top of mine. Christmas parcels arrived on

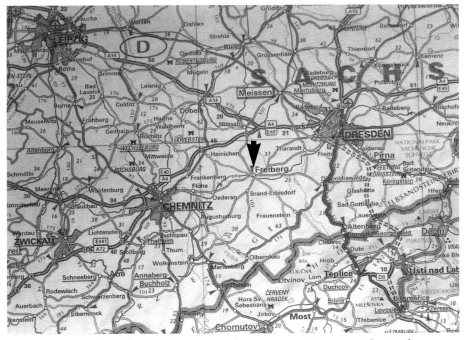

The location of Stalag 4B prisoner of war camp just outside Freiberg, a town which lies between Dresden and Chemnitz, eastern Germany.

12th – and cigarettes. Weather bitterly cold. Wrote first mail home on the 21st. Got paid: we earn 70 phenigs a day. No more parcels yet. – 'Roll on.' On the 25th two weeks issue of Canadian parcels arrived. Our laundry is now sent out. Air alarms are more frequent.

December 1943. It's bitterly cold now, freezing all day. Snow two inches deep, frozen solid. More parcels have arrived and more coming in. No mail from home at all yet. On the 17th I started down the mine, another experience for me. We shall have a white Christmas this year all right. The pay for last month was 34 marks. Funny, the snow has all been washed away. On 21st/22nd had about 5 weeks issue of Canadian parcels. So we had beer and lemonade for Christmas. I had lemonade. The weather is mild and muggy. It's warm below ground. The old year went out with snow again. May I be home in 1944?

> 'As we kneel before the crib of our infant God who silently
> loves, protects and judges mankind, now torn by civil strife,
> may all men once more become brothers in love and concord,
> in the triumph of good over evil, in justice and peace.'
>   *Pope Pius III November 30th 1941.*

1944
Here follows a summary of the months – January to September 1944. The lack of paper at the time caused my jottings to be brief.

January 1944. We start the New Year well. Nearly all of us had our bread ration cut, for not working hard enough for 8 days. Three weeks issue of parcels left. We are still without news, except 'Gen' Central Heating in main hall on 5th. No mail from home. Our planes took one and a half hours to pass one night.

February 1944. Still we carry on. January (1943) hopes not realized. No mail from Home. The last letter I had from Edie was 10th September 1943. Snow still here.

March 1944. On the 1st, five letters for me, 3 from Edie. We have all nationalities here, Jugos, French, Ities, Romanians, Czechs, Russians, Serbs etc. all working. 10 letters all told. Snow still here.

April 1944. We went to the cinema on 7th in Freiberg. Very nice change. On the 6th the mine flooded. We got up OK. P.Ps have commenced to arrive. The walks lately have been very pleasant. Snow vanished.

May 1944. Plenty of work – that's all.

June 1944. Invasion took place on 6th; planes about here more often now. Have heard bombs dropping. The weather is indifferent for the time of year. A sunny day means an air raid. On the 25th we went to the cinema. Show called 'The man who was Sherlock Holmes'.

July 1944. Nothing to say. Rumours of the war are fantastic, as is always in a prison camp.

August 1944. The weather is very hot now. One day about 1,000 planes came over. One crashed 5 or 6 miles away. Some more bombs dropped near here. The news is fairly good; maybe this year will see the end.

September 1944. Red Cross parcels have stopped. Cigs, nil. Some snaps from Edie. The week of 10/16 four successive raids occurred. No parcels or cigarettes up to the 24th. The weather has turned cold and wet again. Now a few parcels have arrived.

October 1944. On the 2nd of the month I received my 50th and 51st letters from home. How nice and optimistic they are. I can only hope their optimism will be justified. In our new 'Zimmer' we now have a most welcome fire stove. By the way, we now have about 300 odd men in the camp, quite a number. We go away to work. On Friday the 6th we had a 'Recce' plane about. On Saturday 7th came the raiders. One stick of bombs fell too close for my liking. There was a continual rumble all around. Apparently, the damage was greater than we thought. On the 8th, bodies were still being recovered. Some of our boys went down removing debris. The weather is lovely now. On Sunday 15th I had to go down removing debris. 3 more letters, all reading as if I should be on my way home. I wish it were true, but somehow I seem to think, not yet. The weather is much colder now. Tomorrow, 22nd, two of my closest pals, Punch and Charlie, leave me. As far as I can gather, they go to Dresden, 36 kilometres away. 40 men in all are going. The 25th signifies 12 months in this camp. Today, the 29th and STILL the war goes on. Will next month bring an end? The weather is wet and cold. On 30th I received my 58th letter. In Italy I had 82 all told. Tomorrow starts a new month. I wonder.

November 1944. My guess at a possible cessation of hostilities is 20th November 1944. At the time I hazarded this date, it wanted 7 weeks to 20th November. On the first, a cigarette parcel arrived for me just in time. The weather is cold and wet. The cigarettes were 200 State Express from the Signals. We work now 2 and 3 Sundays a month. I have never had so much work before. One Sunday off in four. No walks for weeks now. Red Cross parcels, one a fortnight. Sundays, when I'm on afternoon shift, I go down at quarter to three, come up at 11.30pm. Go down again at 6 in the morning, gives me about 4 hours sleep. On 7th, they removed our fire-stoves and its bitterly cold; also no parcels in. What a life! On the 10th I received a clothing parcel: it took over a year to reach me. Addressed to Italy and posted on 16th July 1943. Everything ok. The Red Cross parcel situation is very bad now. We live from week to week, so to speak. Tomorrow is the 20th so my guess is ruled out (cessation of hostilities). We have had two falls of snow so far. On 22nd 2,000 Canadian parcels arrived here. The 25th saw another 'too near' raid. The last few days of the month passed by uneventfully. The German Command here was changed on the 28th.

December 1944. The last month of the year, again spent as a POW. On 2nd our fire-stoves were returned. So on the 3rd we have warmth in the 'Zimmer' again. The work stops now for one day a week, Thursdays, but we do not get a day off. Oh no! We work a double shift to make up for it. The 17th marks my 12 months working down the pit. The cigarette position for me is bad, 25 a week and no private parcel cigs. After Christmas we get 10 a week. I shall have to give up smoking, nothing else for it.

I'm afraid letters are very slow, only two up to the 21st. Air raids, two or three a day. Christmas Eve has arrived with no letter from Edie to cheer me up. We have three days holiday this year. Lets hope (once more) that next year will see me home. The frost is the heaviest I have ever seen, just like snow. Friday 22nd was the coldest day here for 12 years – Brrr!!! For Xmas we had a 'quarter' parcel extra above our fortnightly issue. No Xmas parcels have arrived. Christmas Day dawned bright and sunny. As usual the RAF paid us a visit. This makes my 4th Xmas abroad. Snow fell on 28th laying slightly. Many Happy Returns Edie on your birthday (28th) Snowing on the 31st.

This Year? Next Year? Never?

January 1945. On New Year's Day, the snow has lain at last. Also the confounded water has frozen up. Can't make a cup of tea today. There is very little mail about. Not one this year yet up to the 14th. The snow has lain a little more. The air raids are not so frequent now, I wonder why? Lets hope the war ends this year. Strangely enough the 16th and 17th saw the biggest raids yet. The evening raid alarm went at 9.50; the planes never stopped passing till 11 o'clock. Thank God, they did pass by.

There is not so much snow so far this winter. Still no more mail yet. What news we get is very scanty, some good, some bad. But the end still seems as far away as ever. How cut off one seems when no letters arrive. It seems as if I have never known any other life but this one. Today is the 23rd and still no mail. The 'Gen' is terrific again. Makes one think it will end any day now. On the 28th the French doctor came and we have all been inoculated. It's snowing steadily today. Concerning wood – we are not allowed it, so for warmth we have to get in what we can – on the sly. The month passed without one letter for me.

February 1945. On the 1st I had a letter from Mum and Dad. On the 3rd I felt queer, so had my temperature taken. I am now ill in bed. I was in bed for four days, a lovely rest. On going back to work I found that my Yugo [Yugoslavian] mate was Crank. The mail is very slow still. I have not had a letter since early December from Edie. On the 13th and 14th Dresden near here was very heavily raided. It's no fun being near the receiving end of these huge raids. You sit in the dark, listening to the roar of many planes and wonder and wonder. They messed the power up here. The refugees keep streaming along the road from the east. This week we get our last Red Cross parcels. We haven't had any cigarettes for three weeks. There is still no mail from home. The outlook seems pretty grim. 'Always hungry'. Today is Sunday, 25th we worked all day. Air raids are regular each day now, and are heavy ones. On the 26th we had the last parcel in the camp. The butter issue has been halved. The weather is very mild, no snow at all. The only bright spot – tomorrow brings a new month, – with what?

March 1945. What a country! After a mild February; the 1st brings bitter weather again, with snow falling heavily. Air raids continue regularly once or twice each 24 hours. No parcels! No cigarettes! No mail! No news! – In short, nothing!!! Sunday 11th they have found a few parcels, one between five; otherwise we are hungrier than ever before. Bread has been cut down, that makes it twice as bad. On the 14th I had a letter from Edie, my first from her in three months. It was in December 1944, but very, very welcome. On the 17th we had a raid lasting two hours. A few were apparently dropped locally. On 19th a Red Cross representative came: the usual promises with, I expect, the usual results – i.e. nil. 21 cigarettes per man arrived here from unclaimed p/p parcels. They were very welcome. Air raids still continue, night and day. The 23rd finds me hungry and tobacco less. On 27th I received 3 letters, two from Edie, - all November 1944 mail.

Easter this year, we worked Good Friday and are supposed to have Saturday, Sunday and Monday free. But on Saturday about 60 worked and on Monday another 60 odd go out. Also, for one week we are going to get 250 gms. of bread. What a life! The 'Gen' is still good.

April 1945. Easter Sunday, as I write, the air raid alarm is sounding over Frieburg. I hope Edie is having a pleasant time. On Thursday our confidence man saw his boss and we got a kilo of bread per man. On 4th he went to Hartmansdorf and we may get half a parcel each on Saturday. One more letter from Mum and Dad. On Easter Monday I had to work from 6am–2pm – some holiday! On the 7th Harry went for the parcels, also 25 cigarettes per man. So this Sunday we eat a little more. Raids are now fast and furious. On 14th, we were rudely evacuated (not that we wanted to be.) We went to Dresden in open goods wagons. It is a city of ruins all right. Nobody could have us, and no food. On Sunday 15th we arrived at Purna, 18 km away. Monday 16th, up to now – no food at all. The alarm is on practically continuously. Rations arrived on Monday. We marched 15km to Kenningstien. We have been lucky: as we leave a place it gets bombed. Tuesday 17th saw plenty of aerial activity here. Strafing and bombing, also planes, both ours and Jerry crashing. One of our bombers had its tail shot off. On Wednesday, we were going to move on but now our stay is indefinite. I hope more rations are procurable. Thursday saw a huge raid. We watched the signal to bomb and could actually see the bombs leave the planes. Leaflets were also dropped. News good.

There is a small hope of parcels here, very small – this is a back woodman's life. Shortage of food and water is the big problem. On Friday 20th we moved to a village 17–20km march, named Hellensdorf, still apparently in Saxony. The scenery and folk are much nicer here. Point is, how long shall we be stopping? Saturday saw a nice day. Sunday 22nd raining on and off. No news of the war. The rations are quite good. The lads here are bargaining for food and tobacco. The 23rd – very bad weather and pretty miserable at the moment. 24th – wild rumours of the war ending tomorrow. What a hope! Still raining on and off. 25th – the weather better, but a ration cut. War still on; quiet here though. 'Dear Mum, we are staying on a farm.' Friday 27th and Saturday 28th – just carrying on. Sunday 29th, more rumours than ever concerning the end of the war. We are still at Hellensdorf.

The last month as a POW.

May 1945. Another month. On the 2nd it snowed and is it cold and miserable? Rumour says we move on Thursday for home. I wonder! We did not leave on that Thursday. On Friday 4th at half past eight news came that Germany had laid down her arms. I wonder! Sunday 6th saw a rainy day. A lot of German troops passed on horse-drawn vehicles looking extremely tired and weary. 8th we moved away, walking all day towards Tepslitz, continued strafing and bombing. At Tepslitz some good folk took us in for the night and gave us tobacco. We are now in Czechoslovakia. Today is the 9th. Our boys go by, also Jerry with white flags and armlets. We left Teplitz at 10 o'clock, making for Brux, 25km away. In every town and village the Czechs have assumed control and are using German arms. Russian and Czech flags everywhere.

Today (10th) is my birthday. I am now in a Lager, at Brux, with two bandaged feet. We get BBC news for ex-prisoners here. An American Officer arrived at 2.45pm. At 5.15pm the first lot of sick left, in a Yankee wagon. In the evening we were informed by a contact officer that we shall be away in four days – truly a momentous birthday. On the 11th a large school was opened for us to live in. So now we have running water etc., all civilian comforts except beds. Very nice, but roll on that transport: Home! Home! Home!

On Sunday 13th I saw the M.O. who states I am suffering from malnutrition and put my name on a list for the first transport available. Again, I wonder! For the first time in years I heard the lady BBC announcer's voice over the wireless. It was a treat. In the evening my pals heard Churchill speak. I wonder if Doug (left on the first wagon) has been able to post any mail, I hope so. Today, 14th is the fourth day and we have not moved. Our officer is away to the Americans about transport. Tuesday 15th officer not yet returned, so we do not know. Apparently, we are only allowed to take ourselves by plane home. In other words – no kit etc.

On the 16th at 5 to 11, I left Brux for Karlsbad on a truck and arrived at 2 o'clock west of the town, amongst our forces. On 17th we moved to Egor about 45km. We move tomorrow, we are told, for the 'drome. We have had Yankee rations and cigarettes; they are very good. The weather is very hot. On 18th left Egor for Pilson at 20 to 8, arrived at Pilson aerodrome at 11.20am. We were pelted with flowers by the people of Pilson. A huge notice read – We welcome our Liberators. I had to laugh. I have been grouped and particulars taken and am now just waiting for the plane. We fly 27 to a plane. At 1.15 we took off and I am now in a plane (Dakota)

Landed at Brussels at 5 to 4, left Brussels at 25 to 6 for 'Blighty' in an RAF plane.

Sighted England at 6.25pm, landed at 7pm at of all places, Cranleigh, in Surrey. I am now in camp, about 14 miles from home. (Lindfield, Haywards Heath)

Sunday 20th, after being re-equipped and paid, I left camp for home at last. I finally got to 25a [Grove Street, Brighton] and Edie at 9 o'clock Whit Sunday evening 20th May 1945 – 3 years 10 months 20 days from leaving her after my embarkation leave.

Postscript:
Laurence Seale was granted 'release leave' from 13th January 1946 until 9th March 1946 and 'Overseas leave' from 10th March until 23rd April 1946, these two leaves to run consecutively, a total of 101 days. On the 24th April 1946 he was transferred to the Army Reserves, Class Z.

Laurence Seale was born in Brighton on 10th May 1914 and attended local schools in the Lewes Road area. His parents lived at 101, Bonchurch Road. In later years he bought this house, and in 2001 he was living there on his own – his wife Edith, having passed away some years earlier. Edith and Laurie were married at St. Peter's Church on the 16th November 1940, one of thousands of wartime marriages, and one that was destined to last almost 50 years. He worked for Smith and Brown (clothiers), becoming manager of the smaller branch in Lewes Road and, later, the larger shop in Sydney Street.

Mr. Seale has been very reticent about speaking of his time as a prisoner-of-war, and for many years always deflected any questions put to him about his time in the POW camps. He changed the subject to just about anything to avoid talking about 'his' war. Many years before he had mentioned keeping a diary while he was a prisoner, but I gave up thinking that I would ever set eyes on it.

I was surprised one day about 18 months ago when suddenly he spoke of the war. We had been speaking for a few minutes when I asked him about his diary. He asked me if I was really interested and, when I gave a positive response, produced it. I read through it, telling him that it was a marvellous keepsake. I suggested to him that I make a few notes and perhaps publish it, for I believed it was something of interest and importance.

About this time he was starting to feel unwell, and he was subject to ill health right up to his death. Some weeks after I had seen his diary he asked me if I would like to keep it. I was thrilled. I felt like the cat with the cream.

I bought him a book about the battle of Tobruk, and from that time he seemed more interested in talking about his POW life – or was it that he believed that he might soon pass away and felt that he should partake some of his knowledge?

One day, I was talking about times in the camp and about the subject of food. He said that towards the latter part of his captivity, food, or rather the lack of it, had been a problem. He said that for days on end the meals were as follows: Breakfast: nothing to eat, just black coffee which tasted like beetle juice, and after breakfast it was off to work; Dinner: swede stew and potatoes with the skins still on, and more horrid coffee or water; Tea: just bread, about half of a small loaf between two people.

'Sometimes,' he said, 'I would eat just half of my bread ration and save the rest for breakfast. I didn't do that too often, as by morning the bread was very hard.

I asked about the mine and he said, 'We worked in the mine getting out lead. It was very wet for most of the time and hard work. It was a very deep mine and it took the cage four trips to get us all down and the same when we came up. There were showers there, which you had as soon as you came up, and then you walked back from the mine to the camp surrounded by armed guards. One day, it was a Sunday and several of us were told that we could have the day off: we worked 6 days a week, most of the time. On this day the guards made us go to work, a 10-hour shift down the mine. We went down at midday and finished at 10pm, I had to go down again at 6am, having had very little sleep. We decided to go on strike and refused to work. The guards simply stopped our rations and any food parcels that might arrive until we returned to work. The following day we realised that it was quite futile and we returned to work. It seemed to be to our benefit, as after that we seemed to get a little more food and two days later Red Cross parcels arrived. I don't know whether or not that was purely coincidence.'

Laurence Seale passed away at 3.45am on Sunday 14th July 2002 at the Royal Sussex County Hospital, aged 88 years.

About the Author

David Rowland was born and brought up in Brighton. He lived in a working class terraced house in Grove Street, his playground the streets. The Battle of Britain was played out in the skies above his head, and he witnessed the devastation caused by bombs that fell near to his home. He was at Finsbury Road School throughout the war years, often attending for just half a day. In 1943 came an almost fatal mistake as he watched an aircraft flying low over Brighton town centre, assuming that it was 'one of ours'. It was, in fact, a German Focke-Wulf 190 that had just dropped a large bomb. As he hurried for shelter in Albion Hill it machine-gunned close to where he had stood.

There was little money or food about during these testing times, but neighbours would share their meagre rations, the heartache of death and destruction and, later, the fun and relief of V.E.Day and the street parties that followed. He spent hours in a Morrison shelter, alone with his grandmother, while his father was on the roof of Kemp Town Brewery, fire-watching.

Despite all this, he would agree that he experienced a very exciting childhood, seeing and doing things that, when talked about in this modern world, cause people to gawp in wonder. He knows of many children who were maimed, lost their families and their homes – and who, understandably, did not enjoy their childhood quite as much.

Bibliography

The Narrow Margin, Derek Wood and Derek Dempster.
McGraw-Hill Book Company, New York, Toronto and London, 1961.

Battle of Britain, The Now and Then, ed. William Ramsey
Battle of Britain Prints International, London.

The Brighton Blitz, David Rowland.
S.B.Publications, 1997.

Brighton and Hove Under Fire, compiled by Leslie Cluett
Brighton and Hove Gazette/Southern Publishing Company, 1945.

War in East Sussex
Sussex Express and County Herald, 1945.

Brighton and Hove in Battledress, D.L. Murray
Brighton Herald Ltd, 1946.

History of Brighton Police compiled by Inspector G. Baines
Southern Publishing Co. Ltd, 1968.

Acknowledgements

As always when writing a book, there are many people who have helped with various aspects of its production, and I extend my grateful thanks to them. There were many occasions when, without the help of these people, I would have been forced to omit a number of interesting details.

There is no doubt that the person I must thank above all is Eric Masters. He has written a number of the stories involving several wartime incidents, in particular those that occurred in Portslade. He has talked freely with me and answered my many questions.

I am also very grateful to three members of the Brighton Local Studies Library in Church Street, Sally, Jackie and Owen. They have been most helpful and, with a smile and a cheery word, have worked tirelessly on my behalf. These are people who have a genuine interest in the history of Brighton. I should also like to mention Hove Reference Library who, too, have been very helpful.

Peter Gear helped me to identify a number of streets in Hove where wartime incidents occurred, and I must also not forget those people who have written to me telling of their particular wartime incidents – memories still so fresh in their minds that they could have happened yesterday.

Further mentions to Susie Haworth who has lent me her computer skills and therefore saved me a lot of time; to Jeffrey Graham from J. Sainsbury Plc (Archives) who was an invaluable source of information in regard to the chapter on rationing; and to Ian Wilson, who was of great assistance with the story about the Portslade church, St Michael's All Saints.

My thanks, as ever, go to my wife Christine for putting up with a lounge table full of pictures, sheets of paper and other junk for weeks on end.

Lastly, thanks to my editor, David Arscott, who certainly knows how to put a book together in a very professional manner and who has also been a great source of help with all the practical sides of book publishing.

By the Same Author

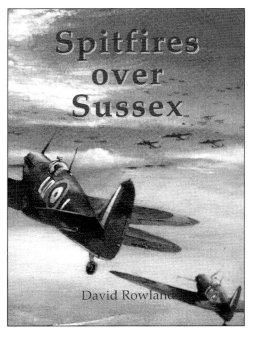

SPITFIRES OVER SUSSEX: the exploits of 602 Squadron

In the late summer and autumn of 1940 our survival as a nation depended upon the bravery of young pilots sent up to engage German Aces in ferocious dogfights over the south coast.

David Rowland's gripping narrative recounts the story of the outstanding 602 Squadron, based at Westhampnett, a small satellite of Tangmere in West Sussex.

Finsbury Publishing
ISBN 0 9539392 0 0

THE COASTAL BLITZ

The story of Newhaven, Seaford and Peacehaven during world war two, recounted through memories of the men and women who lived through the air raids. Includes rare photographs and a vivid account of one of the worst raids in Brighton which unexpectedly came to light after publication of the author's first book, THE BRIGHTON BLITZ.

SB Publications
ISBN 185770 194 1

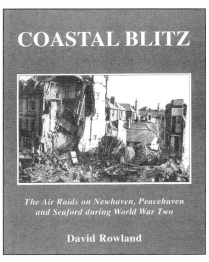

COASTAL BLITZ

The Air Raids on Newhaven, Peacehaven and Seaford during World War Two

David Rowland